I'D RATHER WEAR PAJAMAS

Chelsea Walker Flagg

Copyright © 2015 by Chelsea Walker Flagg

www.chelseaflagg.com

All rights reserved. This book or any portion thereof may not be reproduced or used in any manner whatsoever without the express written permission of the publisher except for the use of brief quotations in a book review.

Published and Printed in the United States

ISBN: 978-0-9967284-0-9 (print)
ISBN: 978-0-9967284-1-6 (ebook)

Cover design by Kelly Angelovic
Author Photo by Merrick Chase
Book Formatting by Polgarus Studio

*Dedicated to my beautiful daughters—
Quincy, Olive, and Pearl.*

*May you always explore and discover
your own definition of strong.*

Contents

CHAPTER 1 1
How to Be Strong Without Doing a Single Pushup, and Other Little Life Cheats

CHAPTER 2 4
Own Your Own Strong

CHAPTER 3 8
Astrology isn't Just for Crazies Anymore. Or Maybe it Still is

CHAPTER 4 13
Animal Lovers Unite

CHAPTER 5 22
Is it Just Me, or Does Everybody Want to Go to Law School?

CHAPTER 6 34
It Takes Skills to Be Professional. And Good Clothes

CHAPTER 7 41
Obligatory Bad Date Story

CHAPTER 8 46
The Boomerang Generation

CHAPTER 9 52
Following Directions is For the Birds. And For People Who Want Things to Turn Out Properly

CHAPTER 10..57
Hangers and Trash

CHAPTER 11..65
What to Do When Your Life Implodes

CHAPTER 12..67
When in Doubt, Get a Dog. Or a Cat. Or a Cat-Dog

CHAPTER 13..74
Game. Set. Match

CHAPTER 14..83
Froggy Went a Courtin'

CHAPTER 15..88
You Don't Just Marry a Person, You Marry a Family. But Not Literally. That'd Be Terribly Confusing

CHAPTER 16..92
Owning a House is Overrated. Unless it's Your Dream House, Then it's Underrated

CHAPTER 17..99
When in Doubt, Elope

CHAPTER 18..110
Be Sure to Get All Your Ducks in a Row

CHAPTER 19..114
Always Give Yourself Plenty of Time to Party

CHAPTER 20..119
Domestic Training isn't For the Weak of Stomach

CHAPTER 21..126
Rhubarb Delight, Wherein "Delight" is a Highly Subjective Term

CHAPTER 22 133
Don't Be Afraid to Get Your Hands Dirty

CHAPTER 23 136
Sew Like the Wind, and Other Poetic, yet Failed, Attempts

CHAPTER 24 146
Forget the Textbooks, Self Discovery is Your Best Tool

CHAPTER 25 148
Growing Babies and Other Normal Abnormalities

CHAPTER 26 153
Talents Can Sometimes Stumble Right into You

CHAPTER 27 157
Stings, Bites, and other Unfortunate Consequences of Pregnancy

CHAPTER 28 165
Oh Boy, Oh Boy, Oh Girl

CHAPTER 29 171
Riding in a Soup Can Has Never Been so Sticky

CHAPTER 30 177
Just When You Think it Can't Get Any Hippier

CHAPTER 31 189
Don't Be Afraid to Stand Up for Your Path

CHAPTER 32 194
Warning: Labor Story Ahead

CHAPTER 33 199
Be Yourself; Everyone Else is Already Taken. ~ Oscar Wilde

CHAPTER 1

How to Be Strong Without Doing a Single Pushup, and Other Little Life Cheats

The word I've wanted to be associated with for as long as I can remember is *strong*. Are you nodding your head enthusiastically because you feel the same way? Good, that means you're reading the right book.

What attracts me to that word, you ask? Maybe it's because I grew up with a kickass mother for a role model who continues to rock the word *strong* every day of her life. (Stay tuned for more on that later.) Or maybe it's because I'm a girl who lives in a world where, regardless of how much progress we've made with sexual equality, women still feel the need to fight to prove themselves adequate to their male counterparts.

But, let's face it, I think the real reason I've always longed to be viewed as strong is because I've never been able to do a single pushup in my entire life. Not a single one. As if gym class isn't painful enough for every student ever; throw in that little nuance and you've got yourself a recipe for ridicule and embarrassment. I'd walk into those dreaded gym periods like I was walking the green mile to my death. The absolute worst was when that splintery rope would be hanging down from the ceiling, taunting me with the realization that it was rope climbing day. You know what I'm talking about, right? Those days couldn't have been painful for just me. You stand in the lineup of students all waiting their turn while watching the poor sucker on the rope trying to scramble his way at least two inches off the floor. You contemplate ways to make yourself sick in order to get a free pass to the nurse's office, but then it's too late and it's your turn. You pray that you don't have a hole in your pants as you mount the rope. And then you get nervous. You get really nervous. Which means that you start spontaneously passing insane amounts of gas—while trying to climb the rope—with all your classmates down wind. I'm getting gassy just thinking about it.

In my own defense, I'm an otherwise athletic person with above average workout habits. Alas, my arm muscles remain nonexistent. At one point, even my mom was worried that maybe I was missing a muscle or two because my arms just didn't seem *right*. As far as I know, all my muscles are there, but I guess I've never confirmed that with doctors.

Join Crossfit, you say? Yeah, I would if I wasn't afraid to get turned away as a hopeless case. Also, I'm scared they might try to make me climb a rope. So, instead I'm spending my free time writing this book, which happens to take very little arm strength. Right up my alley.

Let's not dwell on my arms any longer; it'll only make

me sad—and perplexed. Instead, let's focus on that word again, *strong*.

What does it mean to be strong? Is strength truly defined by the number of pushups a person can do? Is it defined by the number of zeros behind your net worth, or the number of people working underneath you in an office? That was a confusing sentence…obviously, I mean that if you have people literally working underneath your desk, you wield more power.

I spent the first part of my life trying to condition myself to fit into a mold that I viewed as strong. I thought if I became an outspoken business-woman, I would garner insane amounts of respect, admiration, and all the Fruit Loops I could stomach. What, can't a kid dream?

Several years and many failed attempts later, I've found my own strength and changed my definition of the word entirely. I still look at power-house business-women with great amounts of awe and admiration, but I've learned that it's just not *me*. I've learned that *strong* actually equals *true*. Write that down.

Strength comes when you find yourself outside of any of the molds you've been trying to fit into, and then you find the courage to embrace whatever that looks like. In the words of Joseph Campbell, "We must be willing to let go of the life we have planned, so as to have the life that is waiting for us."

We are all capable of being strong. Sometimes we're just conditioning for it in the wrong way.

CHAPTER 2

Own Your Own Strong

Have you ever seen a unicorn in the throes of an identity crises? Yeah, me neither. It's because unicorns are oddballs and they know it. They know that since they were born such bizarre, unique creatures, changing to be something they're not would just be a depressing waste of time.

I'll put my money where my mouth is if anybody can find a group of unicorns sitting around and plotting how they can convince the world that they're actually horses and their horns are just removable headbands they bought for $3.99 at H&M.

No, that's not their style. They own what they are. They proudly show off their magical powers, scatter their rainbow poop all around, and dare people to not believe in them.

Of course, we're not unicorns, so let's bring it down to reality. (Not saying you aren't real, Unicorns. Please don't hurt me with your laser-beam eyes.)

The cool thing about the human race is that every single person is different. I know that sounds like a clichéd t-shirt phrase, but it's true. Every man, woman, boy, and girl has his or her own quirks and preferences, and therefore his or her own unique path that leads to his or her own unique *strong*. Of course, the catch 22 is that every single person is expected to fit in. Don't get me wrong, individualism is applauded and even encouraged, but take the current Hipster fad: in attempting to make a statement and to stand out in a crowd, everybody ends up wearing skinny jeans, shopping at thrift stores, and once again fitting into a mold. No offense to Hipsters; I think you're delightful and love what you've done for moustaches and flower-prints.

The sad truth is that people who truly march to the beat of their own drum are usually looked down upon and questioned for their sanity. Think about it; people who choose to be homeless, people who talk to themselves while walking down the street, full-grown men wearing tutus in public…

"Gee, thanks a lot for bringing that dark cloud into my day," you say as you're crying into your fancy double drip coffee. I know, I know, and I'm sorry. I don't mean to be a downer, but those statements set me up for an easy layup towards my point. So, thanks for sacrificing a couple of happy seconds of your day to give me a good transition.

Once again, *every single person has his or her own perfect path through life*. Therefore, *we cannot all fit into a mold*. I will now stop using italics for emphasis.

Maybe that full-grown man wearing a tutu is so insanely happy because he's living the exact right way for him. Or maybe he lost a bet.

I'm not here to point fingers and tell everyone to stop judging others and to find your own happy. Nagging has never been my strong suit. But, I can tell stories all day long.

So, this is my story. While I can't say I've entirely figured out my own perfect path, I can confidently say that I'm heading in the right direction and that I'm finding my strength more and more each day.

Once upon a time, I longed to be that all-powerful feminist and career chick who everyone loved but also secretly feared. I'd bet most girls in America have, at some time or another, wanted to be that woman. And tons of girls *are* that woman, and my hat goes off to you all, because you are freakin' rockstars.

Not to provide a spoiler alert right out of the gate, but I am *not* that woman. I wish I was a feminist, I love the idea of it. I sometimes dream of spending my days fighting for amazing causes, burning all my bras to prove points, and manufacturing the world's best picket signs to force the world to change for the good. The problem is, I couldn't pick a fight with a butterfly without getting my butt kicked. I like wearing bras too much to do something silly like burn them all (those things are expensive), and I can't even write a straight line on a piece of notebook paper let alone write poignant text on a picket sign. Most importantly, I'm just not wired to have a strong enough opinion about most issues to want to fight for them. I wish I did, but I just don't.

But what I've learned in exploring my unique path is

that even though a butterfly could beat me up, I *am* strong and powerful in my own way. And that's the whole point. Regardless of which path you take, if it's truly *your* path, you'll find your super powers there.

You don't need to read the rest of this book now; I just gave away the whole premise. You're welcome. The only people I require to read this book are my three daughters because I want them to see how fun life can be through self-discovery. They can't say no because they have to do what their mother says. It's a universal law, sorry girls.

CHAPTER 3

Astrology isn't Just for Crazies Anymore.
Or Maybe it Still is

Starting from the very beginning, I was born on March 9. This is important to know for two reasons: First, I take my birthday very seriously and would be flattered if you sent a small gift or something. I'm especially keen on chocolate truffles and little erasers that are shaped like animals. I promise to send a thank you note. Second, it shows that I am a Pisces.

"Yeesh," you're rolling your eyes right now, "this girl goes from talking about unicorn poop to astrology. What a nut job." And you're exactly right, but hang with me anyway. It took me 25 years to accept my stars, aka realize that in the words of Lady Gaga, "baby, you were born this way."

As I've mentioned, growing up with a rockstar mother who encapsulated all thing traditionally *strong*, I scoffed at the definition of a Pisces: emotional, generous, easily-swayed, indecisive…Sounded pretty weak to me.

I didn't want to be emotional or indecisive; I wanted to be straight-forward and unswaying just like my mom.

Plus, I'm pretty sure my mom could easily do at least 71 consecutive pushups. Maybe 72. And that's just the beginning; I'm sitting here trying to think of all the different hats she's worn in my lifetime and I can't come up with a number. From restaurant manager, to interior decorator, to catering company owner, to my own personal favorite—lead singer in a rock band. Truth. I'd like to see anyone try to argue that their mom is cooler. For obvious reasons, I grew up wanting to be my mom.

In general, my childhood was the best. I may as well have grown up on the set of *Full House* minus the two extra dads and the baby sister who was played by a set of twins who grew up to be both adorable and a little bit elf-like with their willowy bodies and giant eyes.

Any little problem that arose in my household could usually be resolved in under a half an hour, and typically ended with a heartfelt hug and some cheesy elevator music cued in the background. My insightful parents left us with well-scripted morals and reasons why it's actually a good thing when your sister spills red nail polish all over your brand new white comforter because it teaches you the valuable lesson of impermanence. It also teaches you that nail polish looks a lot like blood, which makes for a good party trick after ghost stories at sleepovers, but your parents don't need to know about that part.

Without further ado, here's a brief introduction to this storybook family of mine:

My brother, aka *the funny one*. To this day, if he's with a group of people, he subconsciously searches for a higher ground like a mantlepiece, a step, or a tabletop to create a stage of sorts to put on a bit of a stand-up routine. It's impossible to not love the guy. He's found himself appropriately in sales as well as DJ-ing on the side.

My sister, aka *the nice one*. She loathes the word *nice*. Growing up, we'd have annual family reunions where all of the cousins were always required to put on a talent show for the aunts and uncles. As a kid, I thought for sure that someday I'd figure out the point of those talent shows, but I'm here to tell you, well into adulthood, that I still don't understand why they were such a big deal. Meghan, my nice sister, would easily argue that they were simply meant to shame the children.

A family talent show is a really awesome thing for kids who dance, sing, do magic, or can stand on their head for 30 seconds while singing nonsensical songs. Poor Meghan wasn't good at any of that. She was awesome at sports like soccer and basketball, but there was no way my grandma was letting Meghan anywhere near the house with a soccer ball to break all of her antiques. I just assume, as I bet most children do, that my grandparents' house is full of antique things. It's probably not.

So, Meghan would be in a slump, and as we know from Dr. Seuss, unslumping yourself is not easily done. What could she possibly showcase that didn't involve sports? For the week leading up to every family reunion she'd cry and cry over that looming talent show. And every single time, my mom would try to console Meghan by assuring her that her true talent was *being nice*.

I see the validity of this lesson now, but as a kid, announcing on a stage in front of your cousins that your talent is being nice doesn't really make you the popular one in the group.

Moving on. My dad is a gentle giant. He's a big, lovable six-foot-six-inch teddy bear. What kid doesn't want that in their life? Seriously, he's the best. He also happens to be a Pisces, which is completely fitting. Feel free to send him a little birthday gift, too. He'd be honored because that's the kind of guy he is.

I love my family so much it makes me sick, but if you haven't picked up on it, I had (and still have) the biggest crush on my mom. In my eyes, she was *it* when it came to what I wanted to emulate. I envied her persistence, her directness, and even her busy-ness. The irony is she taught us to be true to ourselves, but I didn't want to own what *I* looked like. I didn't want to be a wimpy Pisces. I wanted to be confident and direct like her.

I'd breeze past the astrology section of the newspaper and laugh at the sad Pisces description every time, because in my little mind, that's what strong women did. Strong women did *not*, however, skip the comics page. I know, real newspapers, right?? Call me old.

I'm the one getting the choke-hold by my brother

CHAPTER 4

Animal Lovers Unite

Aside from the typical kid dreams of growing up to be a ballerina or Xena, the Warrior Princess, one of my earliest aspirations was to become a veterinarian. I simply adored animals and considered myself akin to Snow White in my animal-communication skills. And that's why I'd stand in our backyard and sing to the birds every day.

I tried to contain my excitement when my second grade teacher announced that our school's *Professional Day* was coming up and we were all encouraged to dress up as what we wanted to be when we grew up. Now, just try to picture what your local veterinarian looks like and what they might wear on a daily basis to stand out from other occupations. You can't, right?

Some parents had it easy; I mean how hard is it to make your child look like a firefighter or a member of middle management? My poor mom had a bigger task at hand. That's why my costume ended up including a white bathrobe which I think was supposed to be a labcoat and an old pair of tortoise-shell sunglasses (lenses removed). In one hand I carried one of my million stuffed animals and in the other, a clipboard. I'm not entirely sure how a clipboard was going to prove that I was a veterinarian, but I was confident that if the clipboard didn't give it away, the broken sunglasses definitely would. In a low childhood moment for me, not a single person - student or teacher - could guess what I was.

Even with the setback, I still knew I'd be the world's best vet. My favorite animals by far were cats. To give you an idea of how in love with cats I was, imagine the person or thing that you love more than life itself, and then times that love by 100. I think it's fair to use the word *obsessed*. I ate, drank, and breathed cats. Whether it was a cute little stuffed animal or a beach towel with a picture of a ratty cat and the words, "Rawr, what a dish" on it. If it had to do with cats, I simply had to own it. (That towel really existed, by the way. And I really did own it.)

One year, we took a family trip to Disneyland and each of us got to pick out one souvenir. I of course sniffed out a stuffed animal cat in no time flat. The funny thing was, this little stuffie had absolutely nothing to do with anything Disney; it was just a little gray cat that you could easily buy at your local convenience store for under five dollars. I'm not even sure how it got approved to take up real estate on the coveted Disneyland shelves. Probably some kid brought it from home and then left it there by accident. But, did they still charge us an arm and a leg for it? Of course. It wouldn't be Disneyland otherwise.

My parents didn't understand. "Don't you want something related to Disneyland to remember the trip by?"

"No. I want this cat."

"Well, maybe we can keep looking around?"

"No. I want this cat."

We finally came to an agreement wherein I talked my parents into buying me that little stuffie by suggesting that I name the cat *Disney*.

As if it wasn't bad enough already, my obsession only grew worse when we actually got a living, breathing cat. Porscha was an adorable little thing who couldn't keep her legs closed. She had her first litter of kittens before she was even a year old. Now that I'm a parent, I see that we probably should have taken her to *Planned Parenthood* to get her the help and guidance she needed.

Notice I said *first* litter of kittens. My mom took Porscha to the vet as soon as the kittens were born, but they couldn't do anything while she was still lactating. We took her back seconds after weaning, but it was too late, she was already pregnant again. What a tramp.

My siblings and I begged and begged to keep the kittens for the first couple of litters, but we quickly realized that it wasn't worth the battle because right when one set of kittens left the house, a new batch would be on its way.

For a good couple of years, there was a constant stream of kittens coming and going from our ~~kitten factory~~ house. Out of necessity, we all just fell into the routine of raising cats. We'd set up nests for Porscha and help her through her births, then we'd laugh our heads off as the babies started walking or, more realistically, falling down the stairs. We'd create mazes out of pop-cans to test out the cats' IQs and hide the kittens in baskets, then watch poor Porscha freak out when she couldn't figure out where they'd gone. Stuff like that.

The best was the inevitable morning when each litter of kittens would discover that they could climb up my dad's pant leg while he sat and ate breakfast. My dad would drop his toast and start kicking frantically while little fuzz balls rolled out of his pants one by one. I don't know what it was about that right of passage for those little creatures, but that would happen with every. Single. Litter. And it never got old. I'm sure my dad has different levels of fondness for the memory.

Then, one snowy day my brother and I came home from school and started taking off our snow gear in the front hallway. All of a sudden—*squash*—my brother took a step backwards to scoot his boots off and accidentally landed right on a kitten's head.

The kitten started doing backflips like a little circus creature. Literally, one backflip after another—again, and again, and again. If we had iPhones and YouTube back then, a video of that poor cat would have gone viral for sure. We found it wildly amusing, until we realized a little kitten who had never so much as made it through a pop-can maze before, probably wasn't going to spontaneously start backflipping for kicks.

Panic set in. "Mom?!?" We tried to sound casual, but it didn't work. Moms can always see right through stuff like that.

"What's going on?" Mom raced in.

"Umm…" (Little kitten continues doing backflips in the background.)

"What is that cat doing?"

"Umm…"

"What happened?!"

"Umm…" Part of the joy of parenthood is never, EVER getting a straight answer to the most straightforward questions.

At some point, my brother must have confessed to stepping on the kitten's head. Actually, I probably took the heat for him because that's part of the pact in being a little sister. Either way, my mom's eyes widened as she exclaimed, "I think it's having a seizure!" I had no idea what a seizure was and assumed that the cat was merely doing tricks to tell us it wanted a Caesar Salad, which I had to agree, was delicious and trick-worthy.

When my mom solemnly explained that she was going to take the kitten up to her room and make a little bed for it, and that we were not to touch this kitten under any circumstance, we quickly questioned her why. (Another joy of parenthood is constant interrogation.)

Upon explaining to us that this kitten was very badly hurt and probably wouldn't be alive when we woke up in the morning, I lost it. Lost. It. I sobbed for a solid three hours, took a break to eat dinner, and then sobbed through the night.

I didn't dare go into my parent's room in the morning for fear of what I might see. I did however, stand right outside, Jedi-mind-tricking my mom into coming out with the news. She eventually came out, although I don't think it had anything to do with my mind tricks. Lo and behold, the little kitten was marching right behind her, acting completely normal; it was as if it had never even been touched by a boot, let alone squashed in the head by one. It was a miracle!

My sobs of despair were quickly replaced with squeals of joy. Everything was right again in the world. "Yay, we made him better," I cheered. "Just like vets do!"

Then, I noticed my mom's sober face. Uh oh, I knew a lesson was coming. "Sweetie?" she knelt down to my level (never a good sign for a child). "You realize how lucky that kitten is to be alive, right?" I nodded as vigorously as I could, hoping my enthusiasm would keep this lesson positive.

"There are a lot of animals who get hurt and aren't this lucky." I knew where she was heading with this. "Guess who has to be there when animals get hurt and aren't this lucky? A veterinarian. Do you still think that'd be a fun job?" Talk about a buzzkill for a little kid's dreams. It was a cruel wake-up call. Up until that minute, I really just pictured vets running through daisy fields with a thousand cats romping closely behind. Now that I think about it, some responsible adult-figure in my life really should have directed me toward a career at a cat daycare. I guess nobody did because that would have been an even harder costume to figure out for *Professional Day*.

I heard what my mom was saying but I hadn't dreamed

of a life where I wasn't a vet, so I wasn't ready to give that up. I just *knew* in my heart that taking care of sick animals was still a great gig. Lucky for me, I hit on solid gold closely thereafter to help solidify my argument.

The Bookmobile came to my school! Does the Bookmobile even still exist even? Is it even a proper noun? I have no idea…the point is, a giant van full of books comes and parks in school parking lots like a pop-up bookstore. Brilliant, no?

My mom gave us each a handful of coins to pick out one book to buy from the beloved Bookmobile. I searched and searched up and down until I found the perfect book: *Animal Inn* by Virginia Vail. The story was about a little girl who followed her dad, a veterinarian (ahem), around on the job. She got to help out with the animals who came in and got to love on them all day long. I devoured that book in no time flat, then proudly flaunted it to my mom to prove that being a vet was a very, *very* fun job.

I noticed that this delightful read was the first of an entire series and insisted that I needed to own the whole collection. My mom, being the awesome mom that she is, conceded and we began the hunt for *Animal Inn* books. Amazon did not yet exist, so we had to visit actual bookstores. I know. Turns out, not many little kids were as into reading about daughters of veterinarians as I was, so most bookstores had never even heard of the series, let alone carried them.

That made the sweetness of actually finding one of the books that much greater. At some point during our hunt, we pieced together the fact that there were *way* more books in this collection than we had anticipated. No matter, I simply had to have them all. We slowly journeyed on this treasure hunt to find the little gems at odd bookstores, thrift stores, and libraries; picking up one measly book at a time. I didn't dare read the series out of order, so I held off on cracking any of them open until we found book two. Of course, book two was the very last one we picked up several months into our hunt. Finally, I had the entire collection stacked up in my room. It was a beautiful sight to behold.

Without further ado, I made myself a cozy little bed-nest, picked up book two and dove right in. The story was devastating: a poor little collie dog gets hit by a car and is rushed into the vet's office. He's bleeding everywhere and has broken bones and the whole bit. The girl who is the main character cries and cries and doesn't know what to do to help him. I'll save you the suspense and cut to the chase—the dog dies. They killed off the collie. Through big, fat, snotty tears, I slammed the book down and vowed two things right there in my little bed-nest: 1) I would never *ever* be a veterinarian, and 2) I would never *ever* read another *Animal Inn* book. And that's how I ended up having an entire collection of never-read books to sell at our next garage sale. Nobody bought them because everyone else already knew that you shouldn't become a veterinarian.

This is a small percentage of a small percentage of the plethora of cats I had in my life

CHAPTER 5

Is it Just Me, or Does Everybody Want to Go to Law School?

One night while I was in middle school, I came to the family dinner table and boldly announced out of the blue that Bert (of *Sesame Street*'s Bert and Ernie) was *holding Ernie back*. The record player scratched, dinner paused, and my entire family looked up at me completely confused. Their baffled looks didn't discourage me. I continued with my prepared rant about how Ernie was the real show-stopper of the duo, and could do so much more if Bert wasn't around with his negativity and unibrow. I have no idea where these thoughts were stemming from, or why I felt it so important to relay them at that moment, but I just had to get it off my chest. For the record, I still stand by my arguments. Ernie, I know you love Bert, but you could do better. Do you really enjoy finding pigeon poop all around your house? I'm just saying.

Allow me to interject here briefly with some advice for all you parents (and aspiring parents):

1. Please, please, please have family dinners together. You have *no* idea the kind of awesome things your kids

will bring to the conversation.

2. Thank your lucky stars if the biggest rant your middle-schooler comes to the table with is about *Sesame Street*.

After my little episode and a bit of shocked silence from the whole table, my mom started laughing and said, "You're going to make a great attorney someday."

I latched onto that statement like it was a prophecy. I would be a great attorney? *I* would be a great attorney? I would be a great *attorney?* You get the point. If my mom, the greatest of all great and powerful women, saw even an inkling of a strong profession like that in me, I was clearly doing something right. Plus, it gave me something to look forward to since my future had been floundering post shattered-veterinarian-dreams.

I knew becoming an attorney would be hard work, but I was prepared to put in the time and started right away by picking fights. I'm going out on a limb here, but I'd put money on the bet that no description of a Pisces has ever contained the word *fighter*. I practically break out in hives the second I'm involved in any sort of a tiff. In truth, I don't even need to be involved; I hyperventilate the second there's any sort of a tiff within a square mile radius of me. I really don't do well with contention.

That's why I knew I needed practice, since as everyone knows, all attorneys breed contention. (This is not actually a true statement. I feel like maybe my sarcasm was obvious, but I'm clarifying just in case; you know, so I don't get sued.)

I'd pick my fights by asking whoever I happened to be around if they felt like arguing with me. Isn't that kind of me to ask first? Write that down, bullies: the people you pick on may prefer to be asked first if they want to be beat up. Just a bit of free advice. You're welcome.

If my opponent was game for an argument, we'd agree on a topic and would each take a side. Then, we'd debate the topic either until one of us conceded, or until we both got too bored to continue.

It was like my very own debate team and it became a favorite pastime of mine. I know, big time nerd alert.

There were only two people who appreciated that phase in my life. The first being my boyfriend in college, who also happened to be an aspiring attorney. He got a huge kick out of "fighting" with me because he actually *was* the type of person who ran into contention with his fists up. As much as I'd like to remember it differently, I'm pretty sure he won every single argument. He's probably a great attorney today.

The second person who would entertain my antics was my sweetheart of a father. I worked at his office for a summer during college. We'd get in the car together every morning to commute and would take turns picking topics to argue.

Now, let me remind you that my dad is also a Pisces, and therefore also longs for a world with no contention. So, our "arguments" generally sounded a little something like this:

"…and that's why 'Emerson, Lake & Palmer' should

not get nearly the credit you're giving them for being a pivotal band in musical history…" I'd conclude a point.

"Hmmm…That's a really good point you bring up."

"Thank you."

"I can't say that I entirely disagree with you, but let's remember that 'Emerson, Lake & Palmer' are human too and have feelings; and so maybe we shouldn't be so harsh on them and just let them make the music they love."

"Yeah, you're right. I feel a little bit bad for saying such harsh things about them. I mean, they're an okay band. I know you really like them, so sorry if I hurt your feelings, too."

"It's okay, I forgive you and I'm sure they'd forgive you. They seem like those kind of guys."

"Yeah, I hope so."

I'm not sure our arguments were really preparing me for law school, but those car rides with my dad were some of my favorite car rides ever. Probably because we were driving around in our own little sealed off Piscean bubble where contention couldn't exist. Utopia—minus the car exhaust and AM radio that my dad loved listening to.

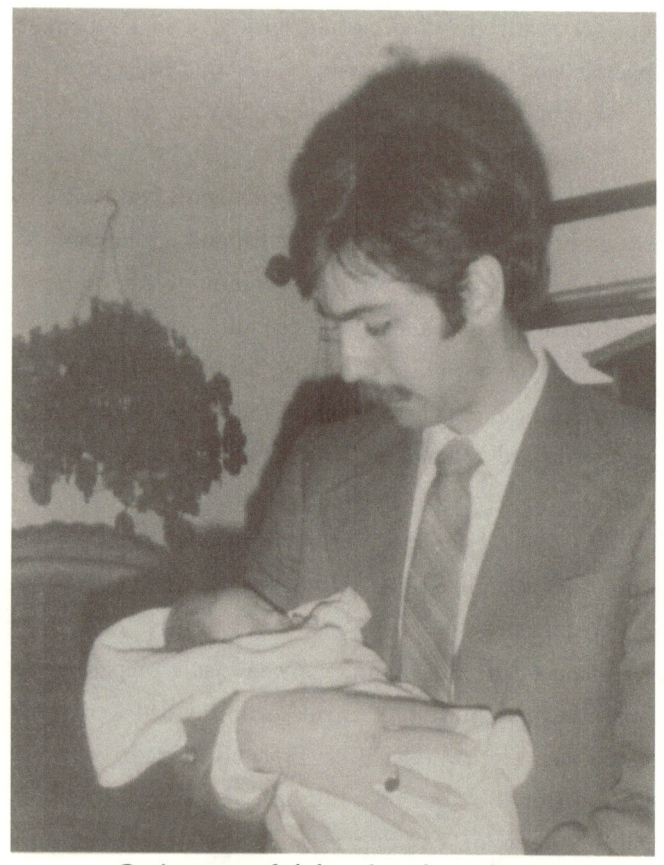

Can't you just feel the calm vibes radiating between me and my dad here?

Come college, I proudly declared my major as "pre-law" to anyone within earshot. I'm pretty sure there wasn't actually anything formal or specific about declaring a pre-law major, but I sure loved saying it. My real major was advertising…it just didn't sound as badass as pre-law. I secretly loved advertising, though. I just couldn't say it out loud for fear of getting labeled *artsy* instead of *strong*. Because, as we all know, the two can't intersect. (Insert sarcasm.)

That's also why I can't say out loud that during my last semester of college, I almost peed my pants when I was picked to be part of a visual arts study abroad program in London. Clearly *not* something a tough pre-law student should be interested in. I know you're feeling mildly offended at my extreme stereotypes here, but I'm over-exaggerating to make a point. It's a writing technique, I think.

We obviously live in a world where there are lots of gray lines, and where you can dabble in a lot of different things without being judged, which is ridiculously awesome. But, I was a young, too-ambitious-for-her-own-good girl trying to find myself and define myself and in that moment, I viewed the world as very black and white.

That's why, even after loving my advertising studies and peeing my pants in London, my mind was still set on auto-pilot toward law school. It never once occurred that maybe I wasn't even excited about law and that maybe I should pursue something in the arts, which clearly spoke to me. The only thing that kept me focused was the belief that I'd be viewed as stronger and more successful if I held a law degree.

Knock knock.

Who's there?

Pizza Delivery Guy.

Pizza Delivery Guy who?

Pizza Delivery Guy who has a law degree but couldn't get a job and now I need to pay off my student loans.

In other words, we put way too much credit in titles, statuses, and stereotypes. Those *strong* words I wanted so badly to capture and turn into my own can't actually attach themselves to anything external, like an occupation. Becoming an attorney would never make me *powerful* or *successful*.

Those strong words can, however, show up internally after two other words exist: *confident* and *happy*. You cannot truly be a strong person if you are not first a confident, happy person. And, you can only become a confident, happy person when you are being totally true to yourself in all aspects of your life.

"What about doctors who hate what they do but make billions of dollars," you ask. I would say, if you hate what you do, you're not successful.

Find what you love to do, people. DO what you love to do. Success and strength and power and whatever other buzz words you want to attach to yourself will seek you out like a balloon to staticky hair *once you're confident and happy*. (Sorry, I said I wouldn't do anymore italics for emphasis. I can't help it, I just really like them.)

Enough about you; let's get back to me and my life before I became such a genius with all these brilliant theories on happiness and billionaire doctors. After graduating, I moved to Washington DC where I knew all my dreams of becoming an attorney would undoubtedly come true. I know they say all your dreams come true in

NYC, but I was too afraid of getting yelled at while ordering a pizza, so DC would have to do. I quickly found a job working as a legal assistant at a boutique intellectual property law firm, which I took to be a good sign. Then, I started successfully studying for the LSAT without falling asleep every time, which I also took to be a good sign.

Only after the fact did I realize that I probably stayed awake during my LSAT studies because of the triple shot lattes I had taken to enjoying simultaneously. So there's that.

I worked directly for two attorneys. The first was a nerdy patent attorney who was bad at small talk, but great at anything that could be considered *billable*. The second was a female trademark and copyright litigator, which meant she'd go to bat in courts for her clients whose ideas were being infringed upon, or essentially copied. She was fantastic and fantastically entertaining. She lived every second of her life as though she had something to prove, and was in it to fight the good fight for female attorneys everywhere to have their voices heard. She had *no* problem speaking her mind, and really, really loved riling things up and ruffling the feathers of the older, more traditional male attorneys around the office. Being directly associated with her made me feel both insanely powerful and embarrassed at the same time.

My days usually looked something like this: Mr. Billable-hours would bring me several forms to fill out that I couldn't even start to understand, because thanks to the nationality of our biggest client, they were always written in Korean. So, I would struggle through a few thousand pages worth of Hangul (Korean script for those of you who don't have immediate access to Google) in serious attempts to complete all the forms before noon, the time we were required to file things with the patent office. Then, I'd turn my attention toward whatever random work the Feminist Trademark Litigator (FTL) had for me, which was always much more entertaining than the Korean patent work. Money-back guarantee. Sometimes I drafted letters to different people who FTL was pissed off at on that particular day. The reasons ranged from serious issues like misrepresentation, to slightly less serious issues like petty back and forth about someone's choice of outfit in court.

FTL's biggest client was a fabric design company that made nothing but Hawaiian prints. I'm actually pretty sure they no longer make anything, but rather spend good chunks of their time suing other companies who copy their designs. For me, it meant perusing catalogues and clothing websites in search of items with designs similar to this company's retired fabrics. How great a job is that, by the way? I was getting paid to look for shirts with palm trees and hibiscus flowers on them. This whole law thing was too good to be true.

My best assignment came when FTL caught wind that a men's underwear line was infringing on our client's design name. She came by and dropped a stack of male lingerie catalogues (yes, they exist) on my desk to go through in search of this name. I spent the better part of a week looking at pictures at mostly-naked men with socks stuffed in their skivvies.

Nobody knew what to do with me. On one hand, studying oiled-up men in scandalous poses just *had* to be against any number of company policies. On the other hand, I was legitimately doing work in an effort to make the law firm money, so they couldn't discourage it. In the end, they just left me alone. And that's how I learned that you can buy men's briefs with pre-padded butt cheeks.

Alas, as funny as my days were, somewhere between polishing up on my Korean and studying banana hammocks, I realized that law actually made me quite uncomfortable. I'm not saying that the world of law is bad, or isn't a perfect career path for lots of other people, it just wasn't fitting me the right way. I didn't like writing nasty-grams to those tiny mom-and-pop companies whose shirt patterns matched our designs. I didn't like pretending to be tough on the phone when somebody called begging for forgiveness for their unintentional infringement. And, I certainly didn't like sorting through thousands of pages of Korean documents. Snooze fest. My hat goes off to all you hard-working attorneys out there fighting for justice in America (and Korea). Keep on keeping on, superheroes, but I won't be joining your ranks.

That didn't stop me from taking the LSAT though, because you can't just quit after putting all those hours into studying. Of course, that's not the real reason I still took the test. I really took the test because I felt confident that I would *nail* it. And, not to brag, but I did.

Taking the test was a mistake because it stroked my ego a little bit, and then my ego said, "Well, I guess it couldn't hurt to just *see* where we'd get into school. Even if we don't become an attorney, we could *tell* everyone where we got accepted to, and that'd be a big feather in our cap."

Being brainwashed by your own ego is a tricky situation, because how do you even snap out of that? I continued down the path of filling out applications and collecting letters of recommendations and the whole bit. Then, right as I was rolling out the stamps to stick on the sealed envelopes, I saw the word LIBERTY across each little stamp and knew I couldn't give my own personal freedom up to something I didn't enjoy.

I made that part up, but that would have been pretty poetic, huh? What really happened is that my ego got tired of dangling a golden watch in front of my hypnotized eyes and I came to. I realized that sending those applications would only prolong an answer I already knew. So instead of mailing my applications, I threw them away. I, of course, ripped all the envelopes open and took all the deposit checks out first because that would buy me a good month's worth of triple shot lattes, now that I was addicted.

People asked me right and left, "yeah, but aren't you at least curious where you might have been accepted?" And I honestly thought, "nope, not even a little bit." I was much more curious to know where my life would lead to now that the neatly laid-out plan I had created as a middle-schooler no longer existed.

For the first time that I could remember, I tiptoed into the ebb and flow of life's running river. I allowed myself to start exploring what it tasted like to actually *be* that Pisces fish I was born to be.

CHAPTER 6

It Takes Skills to Be Professional. And Good Clothes

I wish I could say that I made the decision to drop my law dreams and never look back, but choosing to stop pursuing something you've been chasing since childhood is not an easy thing to do. Similar, I imagine, to how people must feel when they accept that their lifelong goal of losing their virginity to Chris Pine isn't likely going to happen.

It's hard to give up on a dream. I felt lost and unsure, having no clue about what to do next. And that's why I took a job at a different law firm. Turns out, uprooting lifelong missions isn't a one-step process.

I made the justification to myself that this job would be different because:

1. I was hired to be a part of the firm's new marketing team and wouldn't do a lick of legal work.

2. There was all the free chai I could stomach in the break room.

The decision really boiled down to the fact that I adored the HR Manager, Debbie, who interviewed and hired me. She immediately felt like a mother-figure, which

I felt in desperate need of while I floundered through this life change hundreds of miles away from my own mother.

Designated mother-figure aside though, my job was the absolute worst. When a well-oiled machine, such as this long-standing law firm, threw a new cog in the mix, such as an experimental marketing team, it turned out nobody really knew what to do with it. The attorneys had no idea what kind of tasks to assign to me and no interest in figuring it out. Sometimes, I wondered if they even remembered that I worked there. And that's why I spent most of my days playing Sudoku and perfecting the art of chai-making. Watch out, world.

Then one day, I got my big break. My firm announced that we were hosting a party for our local clients, and that *I* would help in coordinating the whole event. I'm not sure whether I was more excited that I finally had something in my to-do box, or that the attorneys actually talked to me and even addressed me by name. I was moving up in the world.

My days were suddenly filled with all sorts of exciting things like trying different tasting menus, picking out centerpieces, and generally just bossing people around. It was like I was getting married, minus a groom and the awkward bridesmaid dresses. I liked the feeling of empowerment, even though I secretly knew I was way in over my unorganized Piscean head. It's hard to walk away from power.

The day of the party, I felt awesome. All my last minute agenda items were coming together smoothly and everything was in place. Alas, all good things must come to an end, and an hour before the party was set to start, Debbie pulled me aside for a little chat.

"What are you going to wear to the party?" She asked in her motherly tone.

"Um…" I looked down at my outfit. I had spent extra time getting ready that morning and intentionally chose an outfit that I thought would be appropriate for the event. Apparently, Debbie didn't think my bright orange H&M camisole covered by a white linen jacket, cheap slacks, and Target sandals was the right choice. In my defense, it was actually a really cute outfit, but it clearly was a little too *cute* and not enough *professional*.

"Oh…okay," she tried to stay calm as she slunk away.

The evening went off without a hitch and everyone had a great time. Everyone but me, that is. I spent the entire evening feeling paranoid that any conversation taking place was about how terrible my outfit looked. I dodged cameras, hid behind plants, and hung out by the food table waaay too long. On the plus-side, one of the members of the live band I hired asked me for my number at the end of the night, so I was at least dressed appropriately to please the band. I made a mental note to not mention that little factoid to Debbie.

The next morning, the entire firm was abuzz about the fun event. Any insecurities about my outfit vanished as the compliments started flying my way. I was once again on top of the world. And then I bumped into Debbie, who greeted me with a giant motherly smile.

"You did such a great job on that event, you deserve a break."

I thanked her hesitantly and braced myself for the catch.

"Some of the other ladies here and I thought we'd take you shopping for some new work clothes today," she said cheerfully.

There it was. Like the good daughter-figure I was in our relationship, I rolled my eyes and started to object, but she stopped me mid-sentence.

"Listen, I think you could use a little lesson in putting together professional outfits. It's nothing to be ashamed of, you're new to the workforce and while you do have a cute style, you're used to dressing like, well, a kid."

I had no words. Which is probably better than having words, because sometimes mother-figures can say things to really rub their daughter-figures the wrong way. Only after the other ladies started congregating did it occur to me that Debbie was not the only one disappointed in my wardrobe choices. And here I thought nobody in the office even knew I was there.

I quickly realized I was outnumbered and that putting up a fight would be futile, but like a dog being cornered by a bunch of bullying kids, I kept a scowl on my face to set up the facade that I could possibly attack at any given second. Then, Debbie strategically mouthed those two sweet words every recent college graduate longs to hear: "my treat." She had me hook, line, and sinker. Why hadn't she mentioned free clothes right upfront? We could have saved ourselves this entire little standoff and could already be out making purchases!

You know the show *What Not to Wear*? Imagine you're on that show, only instead of one or two people shopping with you, you have a gaggle of geese honking at you as they pick up any article of clothing, then stampede by and throw it all in your face to try on.

I walked away with a handful of outfits that even Condoleezza Rice would consider appropriate for the workplace, and admittedly, was even excited the next day to put them on. I couldn't shake the feeling that I was playing dress-up, though. Never in my life had I worn pumps or a skirt suit. I was a Colorado girl who sported flip flops in any weather AND LOVED IT. What in the world was I doing in DC where I was expected to wear jackets every day?

I didn't feel like I was too good for a dress code; it wasn't an entitlement thing at all. Quite the opposite. I felt like a fraud wearing those clothes, it just wasn't *me*. Could I get used to it? Of course. Could I grow to love it even? Yes. But, I knew right there and then that I didn't *want* to get used to wearing pantyhose for eight hours a day while sitting at a desk. I didn't want to grow to love it. I wanted to find something that excited me. That wasn't an entitlement thing, either. I knew I'd have to start from the bottom and do the dirty work in any industry before I *made it*, but I realized while looking at my suit-clad self in the mirror that I wanted to start at the bottom in a situation which excited me.

So, even with the excitement of the gaggle of geese rushing at me for the first few mornings to admire my new outfits, I quit my job (with more confidence and finality this time) and sat down to plan my next move.

I felt a cocktail of emotions. First, disappointment that I would never be that person I aspired to be in my head. I was not cut out to be an attorney, and I wasn't even capable of wearing a suit to work. Second, fear of the unknown. Third, deflated that this track I positioned myself on was a dead end and could never be completed. Fourth, pure and utter relief that I didn't need to spend my entire life doing something I discovered I didn't like to do. God Bless America.

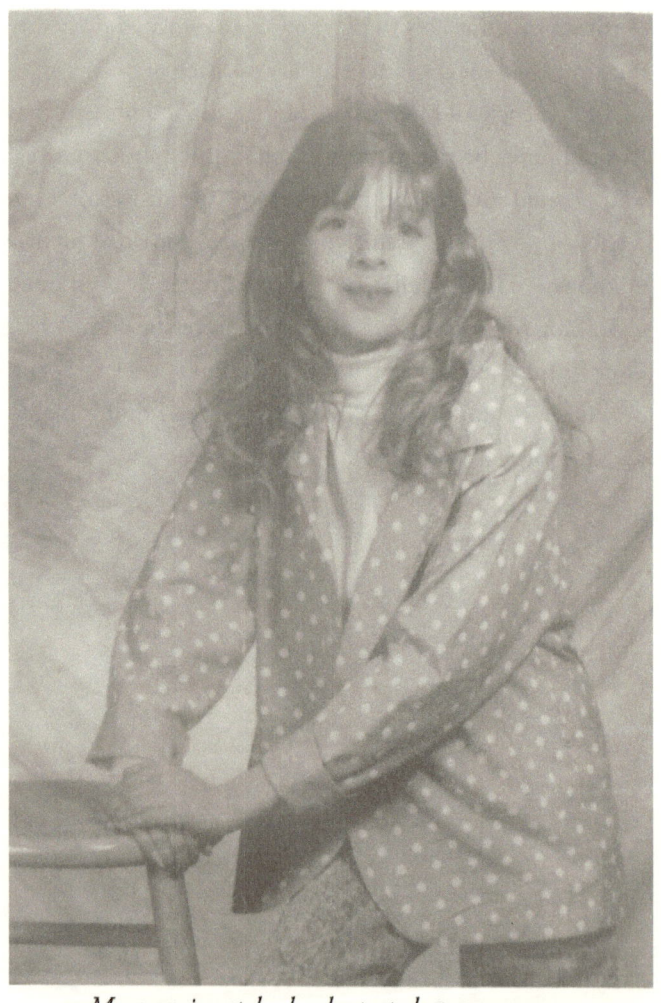

My amazing style clearly started at a young age

CHAPTER 7

Obligatory Bad Date Story

Everybody has at least one awkward dating story. If you don't, chances are that somebody else has an awkward dating story about you. I won't lie, I actually loved getting asked out on dates. I know, old school, right? But, dates are so entertaining! Think about it, you get to spend an evening going somewhere you likely wouldn't go on your own with some random person whose entire intent is to impress you. Plus, free food. That, of course, isn't to say that every date was awesome. Far from it.

While living in DC, I met a guy at the birthday party of a mutual friend who asked me out for the following Friday. Great! That gave me just under a week to imagine and anticipate the delicious free dinner coming my way. The guy was cute enough and smart enough. He was an accountant at some high-profile firm, so he was also really good at counting, which was a plus (pun entirely intended, har har). I gave him my number and he promised to call me in the next couple of days to set up a place and a time for our date.

The morning of our scheduled date, I still hadn't heard

from him. I wasn't too torn up about it; sometimes Friday nights are meant for eating cereal in your pajamas while watching trash tv. I spent the day lusting about which show I'd watch in which pajama pants, and then he called. I was actually disappointed to hear his voice. Take note guys, if you wait until the last minute to confirm plans with someone, you will be less desirable than a bowl of cereal.

He asked if it was okay if he could pick me up because he wanted to surprise me with our evening's events. This was fine by me since I had already done my due diligence with my friends and friends of friends to make sure he was an upstanding citizen. Plus, I really like surprises. I imagined we would go somewhere classy and artsy, but not too artsy. He was an accountant after all.

He picked me up right on time and led me to his car. There, he pulled out a cooler and handed me a sandwich. A sandwich.

This is clearly just a cute gesture, I assured myself. *Like a little appetizer before our big, delicious dinner out.* I even talked myself into believing that it was kind of sweet that he would put the effort into making something for me, even if it was only a sandwich. I opened the top slice of bread to take inventory of the contents and quickly spotted turkey. I had been a proud member of the vegetarian club for years and could sniff out lunch meat from a mile away. No biggie, I started discreetly peeling the turkey off. Then I noticed him staring at me, mouth agape and completely frozen. I smiled.

"What are you doing??" He asked as if I was ripping the upholstery off his car.

"I'm vegetarian. It's no big deal, I like straight up bread just fine."

"You're *WHAT?!*" I felt my neck to make sure a second head hadn't grown out of it that was causing this stir. Nope, still just one. Why was he making such a big deal about this? It really wasn't that unusual.

"Yeah, I don't eat meat."

"What in the world *do* you eat, then?"

"Um….everything but meat…"

He went quiet and started driving, jaw clenched. Our date was off to a wonderful start, if I do say so myself. He quickly broke his own silence by grumbling, half to me, half to himself, about how odd it was that somebody could survive as a vegetarian. Stating my case seemed pointless, so I just shut up and ate my bread. Then, he pulled into a high school parking lot. Wha?? What was going on? He noticed the confusion on my face and explained,

"We're going to see a football game." Wha?

"Oh," I tried to act natural. "Did you go to high school here?"

"No."

"Do you know anybody who goes to high school here?"

"No."

"Are we meeting anybody here?"

"No."

Okay. So, this was just how this date was going to go down. We were attending some random high school's football game, because who wouldn't think that was a fun idea? Besides every person in the free world, that is.

Seconds after sitting down to watch the game, he turned to me with a concerned look on his face. "So, really. What do you eat?"

Was he serious? Couldn't he just drop this already?

"Uh, well, vegetables and grains and fruit. I care for pickles a great deal."

"So, could you eat nachos?"

"Sure. As long as they don't have meat on them." I was shocked by how long it was taking a smart accountant to figure this out.

He hopped up and left without saying anything, then came back with a tray of nachos. I tried to view it as a sweet gesture, but that's hard to do when you're freezing your butt off on cold bleachers while watching high school cheerleaders snap their bubble gum.

We stayed until the very last second of the game even though there was a clear winner before the fourth quarter started, because that's what random people do at football games where they have zero connections. We made our way through the crowd back to his car, and I started dreaming of how warm and cozy my bed would feel about now. He had different plans.

"So, where do vegetarians like you go out for dinner?" He seriously would not let this lay. I gave in and rattled off a handful of my favorite restaurants while he scoffed or made gagging noises with every one.

"Listen, I feel really bad for not feeding you tonight. I

just didn't know…" he confessed. "I want to take you to get some dinner, but I hate all those restaurants you just mentioned."

"It's okay. You fed me plenty. Bread, nachos…I'm not hungry and would really just love to go home now."

Not a sufficient answer, apparently. "Wait! I've got the perfect place to get you some meat-free food." A few minutes later, he pulled into the parking lot of, get this, a 7-11. That's right, a gas station. "There are lots of options here," he said with all the pride in the world. He led me inside and monitored me while I perused the shelves, finally choosing a week-old, stale pretzel and a Slurpee. Dinner of champions. Now content that he had properly fed his vegetarian date, he finally took me home where I popped a handful of Tums and poured myself a bowl of cereal.

CHAPTER 8

The Boomerang Generation

Wardrobe catastrophes and bad dates behind me, I knew one thing for sure: I did not like how it felt when other people tried to tell me how to act, who to be, and who not to be. I was ready to do what made me happy and to steer clear of anybody in my path who scoffed at that. But, what was going to make me happy? What was my new aspiration?

I was 11 years old when the Rom Com classic *Sleepless in Seattle* came out. From the first time I saw it, I wanted to be *her*. The main character, Annie, played by Meg Ryan was adorable. I was infatuated with her sparkly eyes and perfectly disheveled hair. I'm serious. Go watch the movie; you won't believe how sparkly her eyes are. How did she do that? How could *I* do that to my eyes? Same thing with Catherine Zeta-Jones in *The Mask of Zorro*. Sparkly eyes. Must have been a '90s thing.

Anyway, in my young mind, I associated that type of beauty with Seattle. It's ironic because Meg Ryan's character didn't even *live* in Seattle in the movie, she lived in Baltimore. Minor details. I still tucked away in my heart that I would someday find my sparkle in Seattle.

Of course, once the idea of becoming an attorney entered my mind, I had no time for that wistful dreaming, and buried that girly folder deep down into the archives of my brain. Only after the lawyer chronicles self-destructed could I notice that dusty, old file on the forgotten shelf. If the pantyhose and tailored jackets didn't fit me quite right, maybe the disheveled hair would.

It was a big shift in my thinking that brought on a lot of questions. How would I make a living? What would my parents say? Is the unspoken dress-code in Seattle offices plaid flannel shirts? How the hell can Meg Ryan's eyes be so sparkly?

I knew that if I waited around to find answers for all those questions, I would never take the leap. So, I packed up my car and called my sister. "I'm moving to Seattle, want to come?" Without a moment's hesitation, she said yes. She probably had a closet full of plaid flannel shirts just waiting to make their grand debut. A lot of mixed CDs and a couple of speeding tickets later, we reached our destination.

Ready to start our adventure together. After a block, she suggested we travel by car instead of piggyback

Because of our quick decision, we didn't have jobs or a place to live lined up. I did, however, secure some temporary housing at a friend of a friend of a friend's great aunt's house. In other words, we probably had less degrees of separation with Kevin Bacon than we did with this woman.

That's how we met Aunt Billie. Aunt Billie was a woman of the earth. Her husband had passed away some 20 years before; and she had been managing her estate, including over a 10- acre garden, every day since his death. She was in her late 70s, at least. Talk about something to aspire to. As payment for letting us stay in her basement, we offered to help keep up the garden. Aunt Billie graciously accepted, but quickly learned that Meghan and

I both had black thumbs. She kindly asked us to stop "helping" her.

Every morning, we'd get in our car to drive into town where there was an internet cafe to search for jobs. And every morning, Aunt Billie's herd of sheep would bleat like crazy at us and try to jump on our car. They only succeeded a couple of times.

It was September, and Washington was *beautiful*. We were admittedly both pretty lazy in looking for work because we were having so much fun pretending to garden and laughing at the car sheep. It was like our own little sister retreat. Aunt Billie started dropping subtle hints that it was time for us to spread our wings and leave the nest. We were like those boomerang adult children who won't leave their parent's basement. To make it worse, we weren't even contributing anything since being fired from the garden work.

September turned to October, and the infamous Seattle rain started. Within mere days, I panicked. What in the world was I doing in Seattle?! I hated gray skies! The combination of realizing that I was a freeloader, topped with the dreary weather was too much for me to handle, so I packed up the car again and talked Meghan into moving to our home state of Colorado. It was so gorgeously *sunny* there.

Even more mixed CDs and speeding tickets later, we found ourselves in Colorado. Thanks to the spontaneous decision, we had nowhere to live again, so we regained our freeloader status by crashing on a futon in our brother,

Dustin's living room. It's bad enough being a mooch, but it's even worse when your brother lives with his darling wife and two young boys in a tiny two-bedroom apartment.

We were like the grandparents in *Charlie and the Chocolate Factory* who just hung out on a giant bed in the main room of the house all day long. If only we had some pointy little nightcaps and bunny slippers.

My brother and sister-in-law are awesome though, and never once complained (to our faces). And then, we took over their entire apartment with moldy clothes. When we first arrived at Dustin's house, we had decided to leave most of our clothes in the carrier on top of my car instead of bringing them inside. You know, to minimize our footprint. The clothes sat outside for a good week or so, until I finally went out to grab an outfit for a job interview. I unzipped the carrier and almost passed out from the stench that emerged. After driving through rainstorms on our way out of Washington, our carrier must have started to leak. We didn't even think to check it, and instead had left our clothes simmering to moldy perfection in the dark compartment for days.

Dustin didn't have a washer or a dryer in his house, so we dug around in all the couch cushions and gutters we could find in search of quarters. We started washing load after load of our poor clothes at the apartment laundromat, hoping that we could salvage at least a pair or two of underwear. Our expectations were low. We doubled up our efforts by airing out the garments on side tables, beds, countertops…the poor apartment was infested with stinky clothes.

After all the washing was done, we decided to take the incident as a sign. A sign that, get this, we *weren't supposed to leave Seattle.* The rain gods were mad at us and were cursing us for not giving the Pacific Northwest a fair chance. So, we packed up our car *again* (with 50% less clothes thanks to unsalvageable mold) and moved back to Aunt Billie's house. We swore up and down to her that we would start looking for jobs and housing the next day. We brought her new gardening gloves as a peace offering.

Within a couple of weeks, we moved into an apartment complex that constantly reeked of Indian food, and we both landed a job. I still wasn't sure what I wanted to be when I grew up, but I really liked that taste I'd had of event planning at the law firm, so I focused in on that in my job hunt. When that didn't pan out, I took a marketing position instead at an architectural firm where I spent my days proof-reading text about housing projects that the firm had worked on. Only slightly more exciting than sudoku, but hey, when you're young and inexperienced, you gotta start somewhere. At least I got to wear flip flops to work.

CHAPTER 9

Following Directions is For the Birds. And For People Who Want Things to Turn Out Properly

Right when we found our curry-stenched apartment, Meghan came down with a bad cold. I'm not entirely sure it wasn't thanks to our moldy new digs. Please don't think us unsanitary. Due to the moisture, everything in Seattle has a greater tendency to become a bit moldy: woodwork, fruit, the grunge era.

Meghan begged me, "Can we please, *please* buy some furniture for our empty apartment so I don't have to spend my agonizing sick-days on the floor?" She didn't actually say any of this because she spent most of the day sleeping curled up in a sad-looking ball on the ground, but the telepathic message came in loud and clear.

Being the amazingly kind, older sister I am, I told her to suck it up and put some clothes on; we were going to Ikea to get some furniture for her to sleep on.

Ikea is awesome—great prices for cool-looking pieces. (Ikea marketing team, feel free to write a check out directly to me. You're welcome for the product placement and promo.) There are however, two things that aren't so convenient about Ikea:

1. Everything looks normal-sized in the store because it's surrounded by similarly-sized pieces. However, when you bring home only one Ikea item, you'll quickly notice that it is *not* normal-sized, and that it looks like it was intended for a member of the Lollipop Guild instead.
2. You have to build your own furniture.

We came home with a box full of futon and a set of cartoon instructions. Here's a little tip: if you are illiterate (and having this book read to you) you do not actually need to learn to read in order to follow Ikea instructions. As long as you can follow the storyline in a basic comic strip, you can understand their directions. Or, at least I thought so. Our futon had just less than a million little parts that were all supposed to flawlessly come together to create a seating arrangement. There was no way this was going to work. We started in on it anyway, and quickly learned that our couch was only going to sit half an inch off the ground.

This little voice inside my head said, "That's so sweet of you. Here you are trying to help your sister feel better, and instead you force her to go shopping with you and build a couch with you, and for what? For half an inch. She could be happily curled up on the ground sleeping right now."

I told that little voice, "Shut up and pass me the screwdriver."

We worked on that thing all day, trying our best to look as happy as the little cartoon guys on the instruction sheet. But then, as we got to the bottom of our pile of parts, we seemed to have two identical pieces of wood. I grabbed one of the pieces and noticed that it was half an inch too long for where it was supposed to go. I wasn't surprised; with that sketchy box of parts and vague directions, I was actually shocked that we were able to get as far as we had before running into a manufacturing kink.

I couldn't let my sister down now; we *had* to finish this couch, whatever the cost. So, I pushed her sick body back to the car and we drove to the nearest Home Depot, Ikea piece in hand. We found somebody with a power saw, and asked him to trim a half an inch off our little block of wood. He raised an eyebrow, but performed the task anyway and didn't even charge us. He probably figured if we couldn't even cut our own piece of tiny wood, counting out some loose change would just take way too long for it to be worth it.

We raced back home, excited to complete our project. The newly-cut piece fit like a glove. Content with our problem-solving abilities, I reached for the very last piece…and realized it was half an inch too short to fit where it was supposed to fit. I had mistakenly assumed the two last pieces were the same size *without even checking them against each other.* I had mixed up the two last pieces. I. Am. Smart. The part we cut was actually the exact right size. But, now we were left with a block of wood slightly too small to fit. We couldn't finish the couch.

We seriously thought about taking the too-small piece back to Home Depot to see if they could glue on the little bit they had cut off from our other piece, but we were afraid they might back charge us. So, we loaded the almost-built couch into my car, then drove back to Ikea. We put our futon on top of one of those big orange cart things and rolled it into the store. If you've been in an Ikea store, you know that it's a trap. If you go into one door, you'll end up right at the checkout counter, but if you go into the other door, you'll find yourself in a maze that takes you all the way through the showroom before spitting you out at the checkout counters. We chose our door poorly and ended up at the beginning of the maze. The problem at that point was, we couldn't go back out the door to restart because of the massive cart and futon we were pushing; there wasn't enough room to turn it around. So, we journeyed forward. We did our best to maneuver the little walking space in between furniture set-ups while holding onto our futon so it wouldn't fall off, and finally made it to customer service.

We confidently explained to the clerk that we built the whole couch and were left with one tiny piece that was too short. I held up the piece to prove I wasn't lying, even though I clearly was. The clerk kindly smiled at us, and GAVE US A FULL REFUND! I must say, even though their furniture and instructions seem a little bit shaky, Ikea's refund policy is *solid*.

We went back home to our once-again empty apartment. Meghan curled up on the ground and fell asleep.

CHAPTER 10

Hangers and Trash

Meghan was in heaven. She would skip off to her perfect job every morning in her own little ray of sunshine. She'd merrily catch the bus and have lovely little conversations with all of her newly-found "bus buddies," as she called them.

Meanwhile, I was in my own personal hell. I'd trudge to the bus stop in the pouring rain, à la Eeyore, to make my commute with no bus buddy in sight. Thanks to our northern location, I couldn't actually *see* the rain on my walk to the bus stop because it was always pitch dark outside when I left for work. I'd take my silent bus into the city where it would drop me off on the top of the steepest hill. For anyone who's been to Seattle, you know those city hills are ridiculous. Every morning, I'd be tasked with the chore of walking to the very bottom of that hill to my office. Seems like a pretty easy feat since I was going downhill, right? Wrong. You fail to remember that it was undoubtedly pouring rain, which made the sidewalks slicker than an ice rink.

That's why, every single day, without fail, I would slip

and fall flat on my butt. Every. Single. Day. That, my friends, is *not* an exaggeration. I usually timed it just perfectly so I'd fall right in front of the exit of a parking garage where a guaranteed line of cars eager to get out would have to wait while I picked myself up off the ground. Occasionally, the parking attendant would come out of his little booth to help me up, but for the most part, I was on my own. You'd be surprised how hard it is to go from sitting to standing when you're floundering in a puddle of water.

So, every single day, I'd walk into work soaking wet. I think in most cases, something like that would make me laugh. At least I hope I'm a light-hearted enough person that it would. But, on those bleak, wet mornings when I was already feeling as gray as the sky, it made me cry. Not so much because of the actual event, but because when I'd come into work without a dry spot on my body, not a single person would acknowledge me or ask me what had happened.

So, I'd save my falling stories for when I got home. Of course, getting home required trudging back *up* that blasted hill in the rainy darkness to catch my silent bus. Then, I'd wait in our Korma-smelling little apartment for Meghan to come home. The problem was she'd come home all smiles and sunshine about how she had yet another new bus buddy who didn't actually speak any English, but they communicated nonetheless through charades and tongue clicks. And she'd talk about how *never* fell on her way to work, and how all of her coworkers were like a second family.

At that point every evening, I would do what any self-respecting person would do: I'd drown out my sorrows in a giant bowl of buttered noodles and watch *Dawson's Creek*. I'm pretty sure both of those things alone could qualify a person as *depressed*.

I wouldn't admit it, though. I was determined to stick it out because this was my choice, wasn't it? I had made the decision to be there and backing out of yet another life path is certainly not viewed as strong. Plus, where would I go? And then, the universe gave me an out.

One night, it started to *snow*. Now, I'm no meteorologist, but even I knew that snow and Seattle do not belong together. *Great,* I thought, *now that walk to work actually* will *be an ice rink.* But, to my surprise, there would be no going to work the next day. We woke up to the news that the bridge into the city had broken during the night due to heavy snowfall and high winds. Meteorologist or not, I can tell you with 100% certainty that a broken bridge is never a good thing. So, we sat at home and waited. Oh yeah, and ate pasta and watched *Dawson's Creek*. What else could we do? Then, the power went out with no sign of it coming back on. Ever.

When we couldn't stand the waiting any longer, we ventured out into the storm to the grocery store. Up until that point, we hadn't thought much of anything. We grew up with snow storms that caused power outages and road closures all the time. But, to our surprise, nobody else in our town shared our nonchalance. The second we set foot into that grocery store, panic set in. The shelves were essentially empty, and people were literally clawing at each other to collect canned goods and toilet paper. Have you ever noticed how everyone is always in a craze to collect toilet paper during an emergency situation? That's always caught me funny, even though it makes sense; I wouldn't want to be stuck without toilet paper either.

Anyway, we freaked out. These people clearly knew something that we didn't know about what was going on. I found an orphaned pile of firewood and snatched it up like a honey badger snatching up…whatever they like to snatch up. I directed Meghan to not let our cart out of her sight and gave her my full permission to throw punches if anyone tried to steal our wood. She was game. We grabbed up all the cans we could, not even looking at what they were. We couldn't buy toilet paper because it was long gone. We'd just have to use the labels from our soup cans to wipe. Back at home, we kicked into survival mode. Knowing we had to ration, we threw a single log into our fireplace and started up a little flame. Starving after our expedition, we cut open one soup can to share and put it next to the log to heat up. When I say we *cut* it open, I mean we used an army knife to make a hole in the top of the can, because even though a perfectly good can opener was sitting front and center in our kitchen drawer, an army knife just seem more appropriate in this type of situation.

After our meager dinner, we put on our full winter gear and cuddled up together in my bed to keep warm during the long winter night. We shared laughs and tears as we got sentimental with each other, not knowing if we'd even wake up at all the next morning.

Not only did we wake up alive, but we woke up sweating bullets because the power had come back on during the night. After stripping down, we made our way into the living room where we encountered a total train wreck. During our one evening of *emergency mode*, we had completely trashed our apartment. There were empty soup cans and other random bits of garbage strewn about carelessly, firewood scattered throughout, and ashes from our little fire blown everywhere. It looked like a scene out of a war movie. We had clearly given up hope.

Using the snowstorm as leverage, I presented to Meghan the idea that maybe we should move back to Colorado…again. My argument was that if a *bigger* storm happened, nobody would be able to get to us and we wouldn't be able to get anywhere if all the bridges broke. We'd be sitting ducks—likely with no toilet paper. Sensibly speaking, it'd be stupid for us to stay in Seattle. Meghan didn't like the sound of that since she had fallen in love with her little world of sunshine in the Pacific Northwest. But, she knew I was serious and she didn't want to be there alone, so we decided for the second time in three months, to move back to Colorado.

The days leading up to our move back home were not pretty ones. I can count on one hand the number of times Meghan and I have been truly mad with each other. This period was one of those times. It started when I announced to her that maybe I didn't want to move back to Colorado after all because I had just been on a really great first date with this amazing(ly hot) guy. Word of advice: if you are planning on moving in a couple of weeks, maybe you shouldn't go on any first dates. The gods of destiny do not like to be teased like that.

Meghan had already said her tearful goodbyes to all of her bus buddies and her second family at work, and we had literally just signed the documents to sublet our apartment that morning. In other words, suggesting we stay was *not* the right thing to do. So, I guess I understand why, upon hearing my suggestion, Meghan turned on her heel and locked herself in her room for the better part of a day; hard rock blaring angrily through the door. When I made her a card that said "just kidding, let's move for real" with a piece of candy taped to it and slid it under her door as a peace offering, she only turned her music up louder. She didn't talk much to me for the next few days, except for an occasional grunt when I was taking up too much time in the shower.

The morning of our move, I asked the same guy I went on the first date with to help us pack up the car, because yes, I was still seeing him. I know, I know—it wasn't fair to him. Or to Meghan. But, as anyone can empathize, it's just so hard to let go of someone so amazing(ly hot). Turns out, he was not only easy on the eyes, but also an incredible space-planner. I've never seen a car packed so perfectly. Meghan, however, viewed anything he did as poison, and declared his packing job pathetic.

She unloaded every single item from the car, and then in her enraged state, started shoving things back into the car with reckless abandon. We went from being able to see clearly out of the back window, to hardly being able to even see out of the front window. To prove that her packing was superior, she declared that we could fit even more into the car. I not so calmly explained that there was nothing left to put in, and that's when she realized that we weren't taking any of our hangers. Why weren't we taking any of our hangers, dammit?!

I rudely assured her that we could buy new hangers when we got to Colorado, but that wasn't good enough. She marched back into our apartment to collect every single one of our hangers. While she was busy shoving hangers into nooks and crannies in the car, I started in with my own pettiness. If we were taking all of our hangers, we should also bring all of our little trash cans. She made the same rude assurance that we could buy new trash cans when we got to Colorado, but that wasn't good enough. I marched back into our apartment to collect every single one of our trash cans.

Mind you, all this excitement was taking place in our apartment parking lot, so a small crowd of tenants started gathering at a safe distance to watch the spectacle. If I wasn't one of the actors, I probably would have paid admission to see the show, and I would have bought popcorn, too. I can picture the little kids peeking out their windows saying, "Hey Mommy? Why are those angry ladies carrying trash cans filled with hangers? Can we close the curtains because I'm scared."

Once everything—hangers and trash cans included—was shoved safely into our car, we set off in a fury committed to apologize to each other once we had some coffee in us. I dare you to move to Seattle and not become addicted to coffee. We picked up some bottled Frappuccinos from a gas station on our way out of town, but I shook mine a bit too hard and the lid popped right off, dousing Meghan with coffee. Her side of the commitment to apologize quickly disappeared.

And that's how we raced back to sunny Colorado in record time (ironically, not getting a single speeding ticket), not saying a single word to each other. Sadly, it happened to be our mom's birthday that day. Sorry we were too caught up about hangers and trash cans to call, Mom. I'll always feel bad about that.

CHAPTER 11

What to Do When Your Life Implodes

The universe sent me a text message that read: *Congratulations. Every plan you've ever created for yourself (twice) has now exploded right in your face. You've spent your whole life thus far mapping everything out in order to fit into that perfect little box you longed for. You did exactly what your parents, peers, and teachers told you to do. You were sure you had it figured out and that your path was set. Whelp, tough luck. Try again.*

What do you do when the life you planned on living doesn't cooperate? I'll tell you what I did. I pulled out an old school newspaper and I reread my horoscope. Did I glean anything from that? No. But, it was entertaining, nonetheless. What I did discover, though, is that the true magic in life happens at this juncture when you have absolutely nothing planned.

I'd argue that it's only at this vulnerable place where you can honestly strip off all the layers of paint you've been trying to cover yourself in and start fresh. Maybe some of the layers suit you, but lots of them probably don't. Reevaluate your palette. Get rid of colors that don't match. It's not an easy thing to do because, maybe you really like that shade of blue or that hue of green, but some colors just don't look good on certain people.

My mom hates the color blue, she always has. So, I grew up thinking I hated the color blue. But, guess what? I actually love blue. It took me a long time to admit that to myself, but now more than half my wardrobe is blue. And, I look damn good in it, to boot.

Yes, I'm still making a point and not actually talking about literal wardrobe colors (although I wasn't lying about the whole blue thing). Don't worry if other people don't like the palette you've chosen. Not everybody likes how black and yellow look together, but bees and lots of college sports teams feel differently. Don't listen when people call you nuts, or say you're expecting too much or too little out of life. Just do what makes you happy. It's such a simple concept, but so hard to remember sometimes. When you're faced with that juncture, as you will be multiple times throughout your life, the hardest yet best thing for you to do is to just strip down and jump. You'll find it's terribly liberating, albeit a bit breezy.

CHAPTER 12

When in Doubt, Get a Dog.
Or a Cat. Or a Cat-Dog

I'm pretty sure an official law of nature states that the more you declare you're not going to do something, the more likely you are to actually do that thing.

I swore up and down that once I left for college, I would never move back to Colorado. It's not that I didn't absolutely love the state, because I do, but I wanted to blaze my own trail away from my family. Call it a middle-child thing. And that's why, thanks to that official law of nature, I found myself back in Colorado with no plans to leave again. Instead of fighting it like I'd done up to that point, I chose to own it and made the decision to dig my heels in and call it home.

I proudly took a job as an event planner, which I absolutely loved. For the first time in my professional life, I felt fulfilled and in a position that really suited me. I wore flip flops to work, got to mingle with interesting people all day long, and got to coordinate some really cool events. Even though it wasn't at all what I pictured it to be, my life path felt secure again.

So, I got a dog.

In truth, I had no intention of buying a dog, but some of my coworkers were looking at this website that pulled adorable pictures of shelter animals from across the country with heartbreaking captions like, "Save me from being shipped to Korea and made into someone's breakfast." Sorry, that was inappropriate.

I got suckered into perusing the site because, who doesn't love looking at cute pictures of animals? A few pages into my browsing, I saw *him*. The cutest little fuzzball I had ever seen. I simply had to rescue him and make him mine. He could be like my real-life stuffed animal. How had I not fallen victim to this before?

The problems with falling in love with a picture can be many. For example, in the face of such adorableness, you can easily forget that you should probably get your roommate/sister's approval before deciding to buy a dog. You should probably also remember that you live in a tiny apartment with no yard, and puppies don't come potty-trained. Or anything-trained, for that matter. And, you should realize that this dog lives in Kansas.

All of that aside, I think my biggest mistake in buying this puppy was ignoring the name the shelter had given him: Comet. Comet's brother, Gentle Ben, was also on the site. In hindsight, I should have gone with Gentle Ben, but he didn't look nearly as lively/spunky/full-of-character (all bad qualities in a puppy, I've since learned), so my heart stayed set on Comet.

That's why, a couple of weeks later, I drove to the airport to pick up my new puppy, who flew (on my dime) on a commercial airplane to begin his new life with me. I changed his name to Milo based on the character Milo Minderbender in my favorite book *Catch 22*.

Nobody picked up on the *Catch 22* reference. Instead, my entire family teased me about naming my dog after my favorite childhood movie *Milo and Otis*. If you've never seen *Milo and Otis*, you're missing out. It's a documentary of sorts wherein a camera follows a puppy and a kitten around while a man with a British accent makes up a little story about what they like to do together. Just like Animal Planet only fluffier.

The catch is, in the movie, the *cat* is named Milo, not the dog. Subconscious slip on my part? Maybe. You know how we all go through periods in our lives where we really want to separate our current selves from our childhood selves? My biggest challenge in this category was (and continues to be) convincing my family that I am no longer obsessed with cats.

No matter what I say or do, my family will never accept that I do not have the makings to become a crazy cat lady. I can't say I blame them; when your entire childhood has been surrounded by whiskered friends, it's hard for people to view you differently.

Unfortunately, it didn't take long to realize that Milo actually acted more like a cat than a dog. Great. That did not help my case. Despite the fact that I had a cat-dog on my hands, things started off swimmingly. He was such a sweetheart: mellow, cuddly, gentle…and then the drugs they gave him for the flight wore off…

Like the responsible cat-dog owner I was determined to become (and because Meghan was tired of stepping in puppy pee and wearing chewed up shoes), I enrolled him in puppy training. He was a natural. He figured out right away how to sit and how to give me a high-five. Other tricks he came equipped with included ramming into the back of my knees at full speed and making my legs buckle, running at full speed and jumping right into my arms without me even having to bend over, and running at full speed anytime we set foot out of the house for a walk. It became clearer and clearer why the shelter chose to name him Comet, and I started to wonder where Gentle Ben ended up.

On the plus side, Milo actually graduated from puppy kindergarten! I hear some dogs don't, so it felt like a big deal. Maybe I'm just trying to make myself feel better. During the last class, the instructor ceremoniously handed out paper certificates congratulating all the dogs on their accomplishment. Milo intercepted his certificate as it exchanged hands and ripped it to shreds right there on the floor of the training room.

Milo did have lots of admirable qualities, though. For one, he was a saver. He would sniff around the apartment collecting any loose food scraps (or other random items he found interesting) and then would carefully bury said items in slightly different places. Some of my favorites included him burying a roll of clear tape in the dirt, an entire block of parmesan cheese in the couch cushion, and a chicken nugget (dressed with barbecue sauce) in Meghan's hair while she was sleeping one night.

Despite his insane levels of energy, I loved that little rascal as if he were my own child. I groomed him every day, came home from work during lunch to play with him, and even dressed him up—don't laugh. Wait, no, you can laugh.

I worried that he wasn't getting socialized enough, so I reached out and found a Yorkie Meet-up group. Milo was (said to be) a Yorkie/Maltese mix, so I figured he'd fit right in. Turns out, he didn't. In the high school hierarchy of dogs, I'd say that poodles are on the top rung on the *better than you* ladder, but Yorkies are a close second. Those two breeds are like the Mean Girls of their species.

While Milo had Yorkie in him, he *clearly* was not just a Yorkie/Maltese. First of all, Yorkies are like zero pounds.

Milo was 15 pounds. Yorkies like to wear bows in their hair and ride around in purses. Milo looked better in a camo hoodie (yes, I had one) and would only fit in a giant tote bag (yes, I had one).

So, when I took Milo to the Yorkie Meet-up Halloween Party dressed as Jack Sparrow from *Pirates of the Caribbean*, he didn't quite fit in. Per his strength, he ran at full speed in circles around the park *the entire time* while the other little Yorkies calmly sat in their owners' purses dressed like princesses, fairies, and Britney Spears.

Milo at his typical full-speed

I loved that pup for his quirkiness. Talk about owning your own strong. Milo didn't care what anybody thought of him, he just did his thing.

Throughout my life, I had done my fair share of babysitting and things like that, but let's be honest, I did it for the money. Up to that point, I hadn't felt even an inkling of desire to be a caregiver to something, yet here I was letting a dog sleep on my head every night. This new shift made me think that maybe, just maybe, one day I might even want to be a wife and a mother to more than a dog.

CHAPTER 13

Game. Set. Match

Funny how life sets you up. Just as I learned that I could fall in love with another being, even if it was only a dog, my world opened up and challenged me to fall in love with another person.

Without further ado, allow me to introduce to you another big player in my life: my male supermodel husband, Bill. He's not a model for real, but in my eyes, he could be. (Insert pregnant pause to allow reader to make barfing sounds, even though you're all secretly jealous.)

Bill is my perfect complement. He's fantastically quirky and spontaneously belts out his own rendition of The Muppets *Mahna Mahna* song regularly. He's an unconventional thinker and has a thing for sniffing out what's normal or ordinary and then doing the exact opposite. He's a great mix of sweet and thoughtful, but also has a scrappy edge to him and isn't afraid to pick fights. He's a true-blue introvert and is known to just disappear at events ranging from family gatherings to his own birthday party, only to be found an hour later taking a nap. And, of course, he's sexy as all get out…aaand, cue the wind machine to blow through his shiny locks.

It was love at first sight. Okay, fine. ~~Second~~. Thi….You know what? Let's just say our story doesn't follow the blockbuster romance plot. I'll do my best to recount it while channeling my inner Nicholas Sparks. Here's how it all started…

Bill was the president of a company whose software I used at work. Have I lost you, yet? What if I told you he rides around shirtless on a valiant steed while his hair blows in the wind? Glad you're back.

His company was hosting a conference for its clients, so like any dedicated and responsible employee would do, I asked to ~~take three days off work~~ attend the conference. I was immediately impressed with the company's intimate level of customer service, when mere seconds after I signed in, Bill was by my side striking up a friendly conversation. I tried to act professional, but even in my khakis and company-logo polo shirt, I couldn't keep up the facade for too long. Before I knew it, I was showing him pictures of my new puppy on my phone.

To my surprise, Bill didn't miss a beat. It was almost like he was relieved to not have to talk about work and was just as eager as I was to pull out his phone and share pictures of his dog, Teddy. Our banter seemed innocent enough until he said, "Maybe I'll bring Teddy by the conference later and you can meet him." Which is obviously code for, "let's get married and have children together."

I realized then that this guy wasn't just acting friendly with a customer, he was flirting with me. But wait, was I also flirting with him? *GASP!* Just kidding. Of course I was also flirting with him. He was the cute, funny, president of a company who was (acting) interested in looking at pictures of my dog…What else would I be doing at a work conference?

I excused myself before some sort of inappropriate laughing fit overtook me. It wouldn't be the first time; I have a real tendency to laugh when I'm not supposed to—think divorce announcements and when little baby animals fall over.

Bill kept trying to catch my eye during his presentations, and I kept coyly avoiding his because I was a professional (scoff) and I was *not* ready to get married and have kids, thank you very much.

Then, lunch rolled around. Like the nerdy event planner I was, I picked up some data sheets from the hotel's front desk to see what it looked like to host an event there. I won't lie, I just wanted to look at the pictures. Don't we all? (Mental note, add more pictures to this book.) I sat in the back of the courtyard by myself and drooled over the delicious-looking food and what was up with the carpet? Why do all hotel carpets have obnoxious patterns? Suddenly, my concentration was broken with this pickup line—This is verbatim, by the way:

"Are you always this antisocial?"

Quite the charmer.

My response, also verbatim, was "uhhhh…ummm…

errrr....what? I was just...errr...what??"

Which, I'm sure Nicholas Sparks would agree, was the exact right thing to say because Bill invited me to join him and a handful of other clients for dinner that night. Of course, I outwardly poo-pooed the idea, but was inwardly flattered and giddy. You can't just go showing those emotions off, you know?

At the end of the day, our swarm of people made its way to the restaurant of choice. But, in a true act of irony, not a single person in a crowd full of event planners had thought to make a reservation. Of course, I'm excluding myself from this accusation on account of my last-minute-invite status.

No one knew what to do when there were no large tables open for us. It's like everyone had turned off their problem-solving, event planner minds a little too early in the evening.

Luckily, Bill was on it with the perfect solution. He greased the hostess. He *greased the hostess*! Like, in a gangster movie where the mobster shakes some guy's hand and says, "Let's pretend this never happened," and the guy looks down and sees a crisp $100 bill in his hand and he smiles and says to the mobster, "Pretend *what* never happened?" And the mobster says, "Exactly."

I must admit, it would have been kind-of awesome if that's how it went down that night, but in our case, the actors weren't well advised on how to be discreet. After the hostess told Bill there weren't any tables available, she turned her attention to another group of people. That's why she didn't notice Bill dropping a twenty dollar bill onto the hostess stand and making a comment about "if anything happens to come available" wink, wink.

After the cash plopping (technical term), Bill smugly stood back and waited for his table to magically become available. Only, it didn't. Instead, after a couple of minutes with that poor money just lying there unable to live out its intended role in the scene, the hostess finally noticed it and yelled out in a panic, "Oh no! Did somebody leave some money here? Whose twenty dollar bill is this?"

Bill shuffled forward and reclaimed his money, as if it had really been lost and not left intentionally for greasing purposes. To his credit, a table *did* mysteriously open up within minutes of that exchange. What if maybe the twenty dollar bill drop was all just a setup to distract everyone, and then when Bill went to collect it, he secretly snuck a stack of crisp, new hundos to the hostess? I guess I'll never know. Either way, his tactics obviously worked because, not only did he seal a large table for dinner that night, he also sealed himself a wife (spoiler alert).

The next day at the conference, I found myself being lured by yet another suitor: one of Bill's employees. I'm not saying this to brag or anything, it's just part of my story. Plus, I *did* look pretty hot in those khakis. I mean, who doesn't?

In an act of rebellion, this other guy and I ditched the last session of the conference to grab lunch elsewhere. Remember, I'm not the most professional crayon in the box…Nor, admittedly, am I very good at idioms.

We snuck back into the hotel as the conference was wrapping up. The problem was by this point, a lot of people had picked up on the fact that Bill and I spent the majority of the past couple of days making eyes at each other. Even though event planners can't always remember to make restaurant reservations, they sure can be ~~nosy~~ intuitive.

I came back to interrogations:

"What happened to you?"

"Where did you go?"

"Bill's been looking everywhere for you."

"He brought his dog to meet you."

"He even put a tie on his dog for you."

Wha? Bill brought his dog to the end of the meeting to meet me? In a tie? Wow, this guy must have had some serious issues (thought the girl who dressed her dog up as Jack Sparrow for Halloween). Giving myself more credit than I likely deserved, I pictured poor Bill and his dog both slumping out of the hotel in defeat. It was too much to bear. So, I called his office. Looking back on it, I actually can't believe I did that. I guess it just goes to show that you can leave quite an impression by greasing hostesses and dishing out bizarre pickup lines.

At that point, the problem was that he answered right away. I was really hoping for voicemail. Aren't we all always secretly hoping for voicemail? Is that just me?

"Oh hi, um…hi," I stuttered, as if I wasn't the one who just called him. "So, sorry for leaving early today. I hear I missed your dog…yeah, oh you noticed your employee left early, too? Interesting. Yeah, I'd have a chat with him about being more responsible. Anyway, just wanted to say thanks for the great conference and have fun."

I'm not really sure why I would say "have fun." Maybe it was because I knew he was sitting next to a dog in a tie. Everyone knows that Rule #1 of flirting is to play hard to get, so I recommitted myself into following that mantra and intentionally didn't give him any contact information. Boo ya!

Then, a couple of weeks later, I emailed him. So much for Rule #1. In my defense, the email was work-related; I was looking for more sponsors at my upcoming event and felt his company would be a good fit. I was fairly confident that with the right amount of sweetness in my voice, he'd sign up on the spot. And he did. Hook, line, and sinker.

Oddly, I found myself nervous as I was waiting for him to arrive at the event. When he finally came, he went about all of his sponsor responsibilities, but somehow always ended up bumping into me. It was clearly intentional. I thought it was cute and only slightly creepy. A few days after the conference, my boss called me over to his desk, "I need you to check this out," he stated. I looked over his shoulder at an email from a concerned customer who attended the conference:

Dear so-and-so,

I was appalled when I noticed that one of your sponsors seemed to be sexually harassing one of your employees over the course of the conference. Your employee seemed very uncomfortable with him, and he just wouldn't leave her alone. I thought you should know.

Sincerely,

Concerned worrier

"Did you notice anything like this going on?" My boss asked.

"Hmmm. Wow. No. Nothing comes to mind," I stared at an invisible spot on the ground. "I'll ask around, though…"

After that, Bill and I started emailing back and forth pretty regularly. He'd invite me to go hiking with him or something, and I'd come up with some lame excuse why I couldn't. Rule #1 was back in play.

He didn't give up, though. Instead, his emails just got quippier. Instead of asking me out, he'd dangle these fun date ideas in front of me, but then pull them back by saying I wouldn't be interested. That only made me more intrigued by him. Isn't flirting such a funny dance?

Finally, he got me cornered. "I have tickets to this play, but I'm sure it's someone you've never heard of because he doesn't have a top hit on the radio. His name is Shakespeare."

I couldn't help myself from flying off the handle, "I

can't believe you think I'm so uncultured! I'll have you know that I studied in London and spent time in Stratford-Upon-Avon where Shakespeare *lived*, thank you very much! I will not only go with you to this play, but I will prove to you that I know *waaaay* more about theatre and the arts than you ever will! I'm so cultured, I spell 'theatre' with an '-re' instead of an '-er'." So there!"

And that's how we set up our first date.

CHAPTER 14

Froggy Went a Courtin'

The first date went well. Too well. I thought I'd leave the evening with a funny story to share about knowing more about Shakespeare than the boss of this company. Instead, I left wondering when I would get to see him again.

The situation made me nervous, though. At that point in my life, I had accepted that my anticipated career path didn't pan out the way I thought it would, but I hadn't yet challenged the ideals I had in place for my future mate. I had a checklist of qualities that my life partner *had* to possess. First, he had to be Mormon, since I grew up Mormon. Second, he had to be roughly my same age so we could share nostalgic pop culture references. Third through fifth, he had to be at least 6' 2" with glistening blue eyes, and play the guitar. A bonus point, but not necessary, was that he would like cats.

Bill had none of those qualities. He grew up in a Jewish household a decade ahead of me with brown eyes, and could play three chords on a ukulele. Plus he hated cats, so he didn't even score the bonus point.

Alas, something about him held my interest. I couldn't

admit that, though.

So, when he invited me out again, I canceled on him at the last minute saying that Meghan's elbow had blown up to epic proportions and I had to take her to the emergency room. Maybe I thought a broken leg would have been too predictable. I have a little problem with lying, it's called "my lies don't make much sense."

Meanwhile, Bill had his own checklist of ideals that I couldn't stand up to. Yet, here we both were, similarly intrigued with each other. He stayed persistent for a little while, asking me out regularly and accepting that 80% of the time, I'd say no. The 20% of the time that I'd say yes, we'd go out and have a great time.

During one of the times that I said yes, we were out to dinner when he looked me square in the eyes and asked, "Do you ever want to get married?"

I was appalled. Was he asking me to marry him? We hardly knew each other!

"Excuse me?!" I gawked.

"I'm not saying to me, I'm just asking if you ever want to get married, period." Oh, phew.

Of course I had thought about getting married, but it had never been on the top of my to-do list. I always assumed that once my career took off, a husband would just kind-of present himself.

"Yeah, sure, of course. Why?"

"Because you are terrible at relationships." (Insert slap in the face.) "If you ever want to have a healthy relationship, you need to learn how to reciprocate and stop pushing people away. You haven't *once* called to invite me to do anything, AND you take all of my invitations so lightly as though I'm not a boy who's interested in a girl. It takes a lot of energy and effort into deciding to call you and to plan activities that I think you'll like."

"…" thinking in my head, *Oh no, does he know I didn't need to take my sister to the emergency room? But it was such a good cover up.*

"I'm telling you this to help you out with your next relationship because I'm done with whatever this is. I deserve way more than you're giving me."

"…"

That was more or less the scene at our dinner that night. Minus the part when a raccoon tried to jump on our table to steal our food. For real. I've always hated raccoons. I guess I should have taken that as an omen for what the evening had in store.

We walked back to his house in silence. He then saw me to my car, and went inside without much more than a goodbye wave. I sat in the driver's seat relieved that this boy, who didn't match a single criteria on my list, had made such a clean cut of our budding relationship. I was only mildly pissed off that he broke up with me instead of the other way around.

And then, against my own will, I didn't drive away. Instead, I sat in his driveway for 10 minutes processing everything he said. He was right—I was a complete jerk and I owed him an apology. I sighed in resignation, and shamefully walked back to his front door and into his house.

"What are you doing here?" he asked looking hostilely at me over his computer screen.

"I just want to say I'm sorry, and thank you. I needed to hear those things because they're true." I stood there, completely vulnerable and exposed for what felt like forever.

After about a hundred years, he accepted my apology, we made up, and made out. No details necessary. This isn't a *Fifty Shades of Grey* book, people. Geez.

That little checklist of qualities I simply *had* to have in a mate started to dissolve. I realized for the second time in my life that we can't always fabricate what's right or true for us. We can spend our entire lives imagining the mold we want everything to fit into, but we won't ever be happy unless we let go of those ideals and just let life play out.

Of course, I couldn't let go of the mold that easily. I still went back and forth, trying to talk myself out of whatever this connection was that we felt. Bill, the older and wiser of the two of us, said to me one day, "You can try to push *us* away all you want, but we're going to end up together. I know it and you know it. I can be patient."

He was right. The day that I truly fell in love with Bill was a couple of months later, when we went ice skating together. Ice skating, to me, meant wobbly ankles and flailing limbs. Turns out, ice skating to Bill meant serious hardcore hockey skills. This was news to me. Where I could kick his trash in any song lyric competition, he was skating circles around me over, and over, and over again.

I hadn't yet seen him so playful; he was like a little kid out there on the ice. It was so adorable, I wanted to cry. Constantly falling and bruising my butt also made me want to cry, so it was hard to tell what was really fueling that emotion.

Either way, seeing that childlike side of him was the missing link. I realized then that none of those checklist items mattered in the least; what truly mattered to me was that we would have lots and lots of fun together. I suddenly knew that I wanted to grow old with this older, Jewish, cat-hating man. In that moment, there was nothing more clear to me. There continues to be nothing more clear to me.

At the end of that weekend, I mustered up those three simple words everybody longs to hear: "I'm all in."

How could I not fall in love with this?

CHAPTER 15

You Don't Just Marry a Person, You Marry a Family.
But Not Literally. That'd Be Terribly Confusing

Of course, my favorite part about coming into Bill's house was giving him a hug and a kiss, but a close second favorite was finding any excuse to use his Insta-Hot. If you have no idea what I'm talking about right now, you are truly missing out, my friend. An Insta-Hot is a charming little device that attaches to your sink and deposits steamy hot water at the turn of a switch. Did you catch that? *Steamy hot water. Immediately.* Aka, heaven.

"Do you want some tea," I'd casually ask, pretending to be thoughtful or something.

"No thanks," he'd say as I was already filling up two mugs AND a soup pot, just in case, with *immediate steamy hot water*. Bill, being the intuitive guy that he was (and also noticing that every time I was in town, every vessel in his house would suddenly be full of hot water), got me my very own Insta-Hot for my birthday. He shoots, he scores!

Well, it was the perfect gift in the sense that I *immediately* loved it (that word just has to constantly be associated with it). Maybe not such a perfect gift in the sense that I lived in an apartment and couldn't really tear up my rental sink to install anything. Call it a principle thing. Or an I-want-to-get-my-deposit-back thing. Either way.

So, my poor Insta-Hot sat in its box next to the sink asking me every day, "Why? *Why?* I'm supposed to help you *immediately*; instead I'm in this box not helping you. Please, oh please let me fulfill my duties for you." I imagined it might have had a French, Pepé le Pew style accent probably.

While I dreamed about how nice it would be to have instant hot water, and while my Insta-Hot swooned me over and over again in its French accent, my parents were planning a visit to come meet Bill.

We all convened at my apartment, where the device was the first topic of conversation.

"What is *that?*" my mom asked, equally intrigued by its French accent and appalled that a giant box was just hanging out on our kitchen counter.

"It's the Insta-Hot that Bill got me for my birthday." I said longingly.

"Wait? You haven't installed it, yet?" Bill was offended.

"I *can't*. I live in an apartment, remember?" I deflated.

"Well, maybe *you* can't, but I don't live here, so *I* could." If you'll recall my intro of Bill, you'll remember that he is not one for following the rules.

After a lovely dinner out, where my parents and Bill quickly hit it off, we came back to the apartment. Without saying a word, Bill grabbed that giant box and started pulling stuff out. And then, right there in front of the parents of the girl he was planning to marry someday, Bill sat down on my kitchen floor with a wrench and pipe-cutters—yes pipe-cutters—and illegally installed an Insta-Hot into my apartment sink.

The best part was, my parents didn't even bat an eye. They sat at our kitchen table and chatted with Bill the entire time (or rather, chatted with his backside while his head was stuck under the sink). Good thing he wore a belt that day. Plumber's crack might have been a deal breaker (because destroying my rental sink apparently wasn't). It was a surprisingly great first impression.

Alternately, when I met Bill's parents, they flew out from Michigan for a lovely weekend. I'm not sure if Bill intentionally planned it this way so I would have forced interrogation time with his mom and dad, but he mysteriously had a meeting to attend right at the time they needed to leave for the airport to go home. Naturally, I volunteered to drive them the hour to the airport. Seemed like an awesome future-daughter-in-law type thing to do.

Driving your likely future in-laws whom you just met to the airport is, in and of itself, a bit intimidating. Getting pulled over for speeding does not help.

Officer: "Do you know how fast you were going?

Me: "Not really…"

Future father in-law from passenger seat: "It's okay, sir. She's a great girl."

Me: "Awww, thanks."

Officer: "That's nice. Can I see your license and

registration?"

Me: "Of course." (Hands over license and starts digging around for registration. The problem is, I took Bill's car and had *no* idea where the registration card was; it wasn't where it was supposed to be!)

Officer: "Do you have an extra copy in your wallet like you're supposed to?"

Me: "Umm… see the thing is, it's not my car…"

Future father in-law from passenger seat: "It's okay, sir. She's a great girl."

Officer (rolling his eyes *way* back into his head): "Okay, I'm going to go run your license through our system and to see if we have a registration for this car on file."

Me and my future in-laws while waiting for the cop to come back: "…"

Officer: "Looks like you've had a couple of speeding tickets in the past few years, huh?"

Me: "You see, officer, I really didn't like Seattle…"

Officer: "Okay, I'm giving you a ticket for speeding, but will let the fact that you're driving somebody else's car without a registration card pass. Have a nice day."

So, I went from being "our nice future-daughter-in-law" to "our nice future-daughter-in-law with a lead foot." As I dropped them off at the airport, my father-in-law gave me a hug and said, "It's okay. You're a great girl."

And I smiled.

CHAPTER 16

Owning a House is Overrated. Unless it's Your Dream House, Then it's Underrated

While most couples might choose to see a movie together on their date night, that was just far too safe for us. Still not entirely convinced that we were ready to throw our *ideal mate* checklists away, Bill and I liked to challenge our relationship any time we got the chance to try and prove we weren't meant for each other. Romantic, huh? Alas, nothing had worked thus far. In fact, the more we threw roadblocks at our connection, the stronger that connection became. We were falling in love despite ourselves.

In a last-ditch effort to separate from each other, we decided to go house hunting together. It felt like a foolproof breakup plan since Bill was gaga for historic houses while I preferred a more modern style. I just couldn't understand why someone would want to live in a moldy, creaky house over a fresh, clean house that wasn't haunted. There was no way we'd see eye to eye on this and find something we both loved. Scene one: nasty argument Scene two: breakup. Aaand curtain. Yet, against our best attempts to end our relationship, we instead found ourselves propelled forward into a future together.

Less than 20 minutes into our little outing, the second house we drove up to stopped us both in our tracks. Before even setting foot inside, we knew this house was meant to be ours. The sun shone down on it brightly, and a rainbow perfectly framed it while pooping slightly smaller rainbows onto the roof. It proudly stood in the center of the most charming street in all of Boulder.

I'm going to sound like a total new-age hippie here, but I swear that years and years of *future* memories flooded through me the second we opened the front door. I could picture eating brunch on the patio together, our kids running up and down the stairs with their friends, sweeping rainbow poop off our front porch—it was both bizarre and wonderful at the same time. You always hear about how your entire life flashes before your eyes when you look death in the face, but how great to know that the same thing happens when you look LIFE in the face?

For a split second, my mind raced back to my checklists and fought against my heart; this was *not* meant to be my house. My house was brand new with pristine white walls on the cul-de-sac of some prim suburb. Oh yeah, and I was an attorney…How many times did I have to learn that those life paths I had created years ago were not the true me?

In this instance, my heart quickly won the battle though, and I went back to falling in love with this house, even though it was built in the 1880s, and was definitely creeky *and* haunted. What happened to my insistence for all things modern?

I couldn't help it. I suddenly loved historic houses and silently apologized for not giving them a fair chance earlier. The charm and funkiness spoke to me. Then, right as I settled into the idea of living with ghosts, we walked into the renovated part of the house with all the modern conveniences anyone could possibly want. Well, everything except for those bizarre robot vacuums that sense when they're about to bump into something, but I guess you can't have it all.

So, there it was, a house that perfectly suited both me and Bill. Now how were we supposed to get into our scripted argument and break up?

At lunch after our house tour, we gushed on and on about how much we both loved that house. Well, I gushed on and on while Bill, the forever more practical of the two of us, composed himself and reminded me that buying a house together at this stage in our relationship would just be downright crazy.

Yes, the house was awesome, he concurred, but it didn't make sense. I think he was just bummed that a robot vacuum wasn't part of the deal. He got me to agree that this house was not meant for us and that we should both forget about it. We concluded that if we ended up getting married, another perfect locale would present itself. End of conversation. Good night and good luck.

I did a great job holding up my end of the promise for exactly the 45 minutes it took me to drive home. Then I immediately pulled up the realtor website, downloaded all the pictures of the house, and day-dreamingly started Photoshopping new furniture and fresh paint into the spaces. True to my word however, I never talked about the house again. Until one day, when it went under contract.

"Not that I'm checking the website everyday or planning new layouts for the family room, but I saw in passing that the house we liked went under contract." I said casually, bringing it up at dinner that night.

"Oh," he shrugged. "I remember you really liked that house."

That was it. What?! I deleted the Photoshop files when I got home.

Even without that house to look forward to, we accepted that we loved being together and stopped trying to break up. A few months later, Bill proposed. He didn't have a set plan for what the proposal would look like; he just *knew* that he'd *know* when the timing was right.

The day Bill got the ring, it started immediately burning a hole in his pocket. I met him at his house with plans to make the world's best Paella together. Not only had neither of us ever made the rice dish before, but we found a true Spanish recipe and couldn't be bothered with converting the measurements from the metric system, which is how we ended up with about a dozen pounds of Paella.

When you make a dozen pounds of anything, it takes a really long time to cook, so we didn't sit down to eat our (mediocre) Paella until well after dark. Near the end of our dinner, I started yawning giant, massive, dozen-pound yawns.

"Are you tired??" Bill asked a bit too frantically for my comfort.

"Umm....yes." Had he not seen those jaw-popping yawns? I must have looked like that lion at the beginning of an MGM movie.

"Oh, okay. Sorry. Let's go inside." (Because yes, we were eating dinner outside in the pitch dark. We're clever like that.)

He scrambled to clear all the plates while I moseyed in, half asleep. Two seconds later, he suggested that we go back *outside* to sit on the swing hanging under his little grape arbor. I really just wanted to go to bed. But, he took my hand and led me to the swing. Then, without even sitting down, he mumbled something about having to go to the bathroom and ran back *inside*, leaving me in the pitch dark to get eaten alive by raccoons.

A lifetime later, he came back outside, nervously knelt before me, and presented me with the most amazingly gorgeous ring I've ever seen. And then, I laughed at him. I didn't mean to; it was just the emotion that came out.

The look on poor Bill's face was an odd mixture of nervousness, hope, shock, and hurt. I finally pulled myself together enough to throw my arms around him and say, "YES!"

After calling our family and taking a million selfies, we settled down and Bill pulled out another little box. Inside was his mother's wedding ring. She had passed away when he was five, and his father held onto that ring until Bill was ready to get married himself. Two of the diamonds from her ring were missing. Bill pointed to my ring and told me my accent diamonds came from her. It sent shivers down my spine.

Then, we noticed that her ring had an inscription: his parents' initials and the date of their engagement. Unbeknownst to us, their engagement happened to be the exact same day as our engagement. I guess Bill really did *know* that he'd *know* when the right moment was. I felt with all the energy in the world that his mom was giving me permission to marry her only son. It was beautiful.

Adorable, no?

The next day, still floating from the engagement, we went for a little walk around town. I didn't realize where

Bill was taking me until we passed by that same old house that I had memorized inside and out.

"Oh, you're just being cruel," I pouted when he pointed out the "SOLD" sign in the front yard.

"Hey, let's go knock on the door and see if anyone's home. I wonder what type of people ended up buying it?"

After a few tries with nobody answering, Bill did what any sensible person (who wanted to die in a cheesy horror movie) would do and pushed open the door.

"Hello?" He called into the empty hallways. I stood back fitting all the pieces together in my mind.

"Wait a minute..." I hit my Eureka moment. "*YOU* bought this house?"

Like a little kid (with enough money to purchase a house), Bill cheered, "No, *WE* bought the house. It's ours!"

I didn't laugh in his face that time. Instead I cried. I cried because, even though my checklists were not anywhere close to being crossed off, there was no way in the universe my life could be any more perfect than it was in that moment.

CHAPTER 17

When in Doubt, Elope

Next checklist to completely ignore? The wedding.

I have to be honest, unlike most little girls, I had never actually put much thought into what my wedding would look like. Well, except I knew that I wanted my colors to be light green and dark green. And I wanted massively tall vases holding calla lilies for my table centerpieces. And I wanted to wear a white top hat. And…okay, fine. I guess I did have a pretty solid picture in my mind of what my big day would look like.

But, when the task was upon me to actually plan the special event, I found myself floundering terribly. Pathetic given I was an event planner, huh?

But come on, how in the world were we going to celebrate both religious traditions without doing full-on ceremonies of one or the other? How would our families get along? Would they bicker and try to talk us out of marrying each other because of our different upbringings? What if my grandparents found out we were living together before marriage? How would our guests talk to each other across the table if there were giant vases full of calla lilies blocking their line of sight?

I'm trying to remember what felt so dramatic and unfathomable about any of these questions, but the only three words that come to mind are First, and World, and Problems. Anyway, these issues were *real*, people! At least in my mind they were. I couldn't wrap my head around any of it, and meanwhile started driving everyone associated with me crazy.

Bill was supportive of whatever I wanted to do. Unless it wasn't what he wanted to do and then he'd veto the idea and I'd start back at the drawing board.

My mom, and sounding board, stayed blessedly patient with me and took my daily phone calls of changes to the plan with stride. I'd call and blubber on about how we wanted to get married in our new, lovely house but we couldn't possibly fit ten thousand people there, so maybe we should just invite two people a piece.

Three days later, I'd insist that we needed ten thousand people at our wedding and we may as well rent out the biggest church we could find. But wait…which denomination of church would we rent? Scratch that idea. We couldn't rent a church *or* invite ten thousand people. Maybe we could rent a yurt? First. World. Problems.

One day, my mom finally stopped me mid-rant with a simple solution, "Why don't you guys travel somewhere exotic and just get the marriage part over with? Then you can have a party when you get home and be relaxed with the whole thing."

The heavens opened and choirs of angels (both

Mormon and Jewish ones) sang glorious Hallelujahs. Did my mother really just recommend we elope? Yes, yes she did. Best mom ever.

Never in my wildest dreams would I have envisioned a wedding that involved eloping. But, I was starting to get used to this bucking-my-expectations thing, so we shrugged and went along with it. We both looked at our "places to visit" lists and quickly agreed on New Zealand. We determined that the best time to go was in February. At the time, it was the first week of January.

My mom, once again proving her rockstar-ness, flew up within days and took me dress shopping. The Mormon/Jewish angels sang once again, when sitting front and center in the first store we looked at hung the perfect beach gown that would be easy to travel with and fit me perfectly off the rack. So what if I didn't wear a white top hat?

I paid extra close attention to filling out all the proper forms necessary to get married in New Zealand. I even called the U.S. Social Security Office to see if we would also have to get a U.S. wedding certificate to make it legal in the States. I wasn't entirely sure they were the right people to talk to, but since I likely couldn't get a hold of President Obama himself, it seemed like a good place to start. They assured me that as long as our out-of-country certificate was in English, it counted. My level of organization shocked even myself.

Next up was finding somebody to marry us once we got to NZ. Bill was cool with having a Mormon bishop performing the ceremony, and I didn't complain since Mormons are known for their awesomely easy-to-access communities worldwide. I quickly found someone willing to marry us, but learned that technology in New Zealand is about 30 years behind, so cell phones and emailing hadn't been invented there yet. That meant, actually communicating with this bishop about details would be next to impossible. We agreed that it would be best to just meet up as soon as we got to the country to firm up the specifics of our big day.

Finally, I secured a little homestay at what was considered to be one of the most beautiful beaches on the island where we could sleep for our pre- and post-wedding nights. The owner of this home was tickled pink to host us, and eagerly agreed to stand in with her husband as witnesses to our marriage.

Once again, most of this happened over land-lines with no email confirmations or receipts of any kind, so I wasn't *entirely* sure anything was actually lined up. Even still, I was hugely impressed with my awesome administration skills. (Pause for audience admiration and applause.)

Things started off a bit rocky. The day of our flight, my mom came back into town just to drive us to the airport. Can I please just interject once again how amazing that is? She willingly *drove* us to the airport to wave goodbye as we boarded a plane to get married without her. I have to say, I sort of hate myself for doing that. She should have been there. That's one of the biggest regrets in my life—sorry for the sentiment (wipes eyes with tissue).

Anyway, we didn't leave for the airport nearly as early as we should have because my silly husband-to-be spent an impressive amount of time wandering around the house shoving random things into his suitcase to take on the trip. This, by the way, is totally uncharacteristic of him. I think the longest I've ever seen him take to pack for a trip is three minutes. tops. I figured he was just feeling some jitters and didn't rush him. After watching him pack his ukulele though, I knew he was losing his mind and urged him to wrap it up so we could get going.

My mom was flying down the highway to get us to the airport in time. Then, she got pulled over. I think it was by the same cop who pulled me over when I drove my in-laws to the airport. I started wondering if the choir of angels decided this wasn't a good idea after all.

At the airport, we begged people in the security line to let us go first, then ran at full speed to our gate. Picture this: two people sprinting to catch a flight while pulling luggage behind them (we missed the timeframe to check our bags…that's how late we were), holding onto a wedding dress, a suit, backpacks, two full-sized pillows, and a ukulele. It's a miracle we didn't find ourselves on YouTube with the label #airportvirgins.

Then, as anybody who's experienced it can attest to, the worst thing that could happen at an airport happened: the doors for our gate STARTED TO CLOSE! Once those doors close, you're screwed. At that point, there's no way you're getting on your flight no matter how much you beg or bribe.

Luckily, we had an ace up our sleeve. I ran to the gate agent holding up my wedding dress up and panted, "Please tell me we can still get on this flight. I'm supposed to get married in New Zealand in two days, and if we don't make this flight, it's not going to happen." I was pretty sure that wasn't true, but desperate times call for desperate measures.

The gate agent stopped me short, reopened the door, and whispered a sneaky "Congratulations!" The choir of angels came back in full force.

Fast-forward an impressively long flight, and we arrived safely in New Zealand where we rented a lovely little camper van and drove to the courthouse to pick up our wedding license. The "certificate" looked more like a 1980s voter registration form. I think it was even printed on carbon copy paper. The dazzling goldenrod hue of the paper was the cherry on top.

We stopped ourselves from questioning the legitimacy of the document, and instead paid the dues and made our way to our next stop: meeting with the bishop. We followed the map to the address he had given me and ended up in the New Zealand equivalent of a *Dicks Sporting Goods* store. The man marrying us sold Nike High Tops for a living.

After being paged over the loudspeaker, the bishop appeared in his company polo and khakis. He shyly introduced himself then asked his manager if there was a quiet place we could talk for a few minutes. The manager ushered us back to the utility closet.

I waited for the bishop to start the conversation, but he wasn't making a move to, so I spoke up.

"So, thanks for agreeing to marry us."

"Sure." He wasn't much of a talker. He wasn't the rude kind of quiet. He was just the quiet kind of quiet.

"We were hoping to go over some of the logistics of how the ceremony would look."

"Okay."

"We want to get married on the beach, so maybe you can come to the house where we're staying and we can all head down to the beach?"

"Okay."

"Cool. Is there anything else we should talk about?"

"Nice weather we're having, huh?"

"Yes it is. I'm very glad we met."

We walked out of there, puke-colored certificate in hand, without any more confidence than we'd had the previous day that this marriage was actually going to happen. We journeyed forward anyway and found our way to our designated host home. Nobody answered. After a string of knocks, each getting more desperate, a gruff-looking older man finally opened the door. I smiled as enthusiastically as I did on picture days in elementary school, but this man just glared at me. This was not what I had expected.

He grunted something or another about coming inside and then retreated back to his La-Z-boy, leaving us standing in the entry way not knowing what to do. And that was our first impression of Martin. We later learned (from his wife) that Martin was a retired sheep farmer who loved the solitary lifestyle, but promised his wife she could live out her dream of owning a bed and breakfast once he left his life with sheep. Long story short, conversation was not his forté.

Not more than a couple of minutes later, Diane came bursting in to break the awkward silence. She was the complete antithesis of Martin. She squealed and grabbed me in a full-body hug before even introducing herself. "I'm SO excited to have you here! We've never had a *bride* stay with us before! Can I help you get ready? Can I see your dress? I'm so excited! What can I get for you? You're beautiful!" I liked Diane.

She set us up in the *honeymoon suite.* It was actually just her son's old bedroom, but for us, it got a special title.

There was another set of guests staying at the house: two tiny Asian women who didn't speak a lick of English, so they had no idea they would become part of a wedding the next day. They really, *really* loved to smile and give thumbs up.

That night, I tossed and turned instead of sleeping. Dreams came and went where I couldn't get my dress on right, or I couldn't get my hair and makeup to look good. Or, even worse, a giant wave of CoolWhip overtook our ceremony and drowned us all.

I started panicking. What if nobody was there to take pictures of us? What if nobody was even there to stand witness for us? Why were we doing this? We were going into the biggest day of our lives with no moral support.

Why couldn't we just suck it up and figure out how to have a normal wedding? At least then we wouldn't drown in an ocean of CoolWhip.

Then, in my fleeting dreams, my mom and sister—my two best friends—showed up. They brought makeup and curling irons and took matters into their own hands, tying my dress, applying my mascara, and loving on me the way any bride wants to be loved on, whether or not she will ever admit it. My best friends gave me a big hug and a kiss when they were done making me look magnificent and told me it was all going to be wonderful. I drifted off into a peaceful sleep after that.

When I woke up, Diane was waiting right outside our door, bubbling with excitement for the day. She told me she had invited her daughter-in-law over to help me get ready and to take pictures, if I didn't mind. Of *course* I didn't mind! I silently thanked my mom and sister for sending angels to help me.

While I was getting into my dress and doing my hair, Bill was downstairs, as pale as a ghost. He hadn't anticipated feeling nervous, especially since the whole deal was so low-key. But, his nerves got the best of him anyway, and he wished for moral support, too. From his silent corner of the room, gruff old Martin took notice and spoke up, "Looks like you need a little something to calm your nerves. Everything's going to be great." He came over and poured Bill some sort of mystery shot to take the edge off. Even the toughest of men can be the perfect comfort.

Then Bill and Martin walked down to the beach to

wait for me. I came downstairs feeling like a million bucks to find a bouquet of fresh New Zealand flowers that Bill and Diane had put together for me. It was just as gorgeous as I felt. May every girl feel gorgeous on her wedding day, whatever her wedding day looks like.

As I walked the street in this little New Zealand neighborhood, people started coming out of their houses to watch me, cheer for me, and to take pictures. May every bride feel like a celebrity on her wedding day, whatever her wedding day looks like.

This whole train of people followed me down to the beach where my husband-to-be was waiting, ukulele in hand. So *that's* why he brought the ukulele! My non-musical husband had secretly spent the weeks prior learning to play "Somewhere over the Rainbow" for me at the beach as a wedding gift.

It was the best rendition of the song I'd ever heard.

With the man I loved more than anything in the world in front of me, and a congregation of complete strangers, undoubtedly sent by my mom and sister's spirits, we started in on the perfect little wedding ceremony that looked nothing like what I ever pictured it would.

Our bishop totally showed up and gave a beautiful, albeit very quiet, little sermon for us. Then, as if that wasn't enough, the congregation of strangers started singing a native wedding song while collecting a boxful of shells to gift to us.

I never could have imagined that that's what my wedding day would look like. Eloping to New Zealand with my Jewish husband was certainly *not* part of the plan. Yet, there I was, having the exact right experience for me. It was pure magic.

And then we got eaten alive by sand flies.

CHAPTER 18

Be Sure to Get All Your Ducks in a Row

After touring around New Zealand for a couple of weeks, we made the impressively long flight back home where and I hit the ground running to change my name. I really wasn't in any huge hurry to have a new name. I was more just interested to see if I actually *could* change my name with this 1980s goldenrod voter form the Kiwis called a wedding license.

Some women are really adamant about keeping their maiden name and others wholeheartedly want to take on their husbands' names. I'm a respecter of both sides, but my favorite story has got to be our neighbor, who felt it unfair that if a name change *did* happen with a marriage, it was just assumed to be the wife taking on the husband's name. Why couldn't a man take on a woman's name for a change?

Her fiancé didn't care one way or the other, so they tied a doggie treat to two separate pieces of paper, one piece with his last name written on it and one piece with hers. Then, at their wedding—I'm not making this up—they invited their dog to come up and choose the treat he wanted. Whichever name was attached to the treat their dog chose would become their joint name. The dog chose her last name.

I like to imagine the Father-of-the-Groom in this situation. I picture him as this traditional man's man in a nice suit with a little pink boutonniere, trying to keep his cool and not reach for his flask as he watches a hungry dog snuff out his family name.

Anyway, I just always planned to take on my husband's last name. Call me old-fashioned. Whatever. I went to the Social Security Office with baited breath. Would they really let me change my name based solely on this yellow piece of paper? There was no way I was actually going to get away with this. Twelve and a half hours later, my number was finally called and I presented my carbon copy original to the girl at the counter. She glared at me, not because she was mean but because that's what employees at places like that are trained to do, and then signed off on a new form granting my name change. Yes! I love you, America!

Knowing the hardest hurdle was behind me, I skipped all the way to the DMV to get a new driver's license. Bill needed to renew his as well, so we went together. Although, he preferred to gallop while I skipped. There's good camaraderie in having a friend with you at the DMV because it not only gives you someone to talk to during the three hour wait, but there's also a sick satisfaction that some other sucker you know is wasting a good chunk of their day, too.

We sat and laughed while watching the official driver's license camera guy direct person after person to stop smiling and look uglier while he snapped each picture. When it was finally my turn, a zitty teenager called me up and asked, "What are you in for?" It seemed like appropriate wording given I would soon be standing in front of that camera guy to take my own ~~mug shot~~ driver's license photo.

I told the pimply kid that "I was in for" changing my name. He flipped through my documents and stated, "You need an American wedding license to do this."

"Uh, I don't think so," I scoffed. "I'll have you know that I just went through all of that with the Social Security Office. THE Social Security Office."

He was not impressed with my name-dropping. "Listen, lady. Our rules here say that you need an American wedding license. End of story."

I was not happy. Didn't he realize that I was a newlywed and could have spent the last three hours having sex with my new husband instead of waiting in this line?

"Here are your options," he didn't notice my frustration as he recited perfectly from memory, "You can go to the courthouse and get a marriage license there, or you can bring your husband back here and we can fill out a common-law marriage license for you."

"Oh perfect! My husband happens to already be here! Who do we need to talk to to sign that document right now?"

"I can do it," said the kid, who likely couldn't even grow a moustache yet. I called Bill over and we held hands while this guy, through occasional puberty voice squeaks, essentially married us.

I'm pretty sure the other fifty or so people in the waiting room of the DMV had no idea that they were just witnesses to a marriage. At least I hope they had no idea because nobody even said congratulations, which would just have been downright rude if they knew.

So, we technically got married twice and have two documents to show for it. Turns out a common law marriage license isn't much prettier than a New Zealand wedding certificate. At least it's on white paper.

CHAPTER 19

Always Give Yourself Plenty of Time to Party

We figured that if we weren't legally married in at least one country by this point, it was no fault of ours so we turned our attention to planning our grand party. Let me interject quickly that I know I'm starting to stray a bit from my whole premise of finding your own path in life (call it a Pisces thing), but these are fun stories nonetheless, so you'll just have to grin and bear it. I promise I'll circle back around at some point.

Ever since we stepped foot into *our* house on that emotional day, we knew the wedding celebration would be held there. We also figured we'd invite everyone under the sun, because, why not? Since it wasn't a *real* wedding, chances were not as many people would show up. Finally, we knew we wanted good food.

I started calling caterers, but realized immediately that I had made a mistake: I told the caterers we were planning a *wedding* celebration. The word *wedding* alone marks up catering prices a million fold. Let that be a word of wisdom to everyone out there. Just call it a random-gathering-for-no-apparent-reason-where-one-person-maybe-wearing-a-white-dress. You're welcome.

One caterer stood out above the rest in my mind, so he and I agreed on a menu and he agreed to get back to me within a few days with pricing. I liked him, he was nice. Sure enough, a few days (plus three weeks) later, he finally got back to me. His prices were ridiculously astronomical and felt just downright offensive. I suddenly liked him a lot less. It left me in quite a pickle since our wedding party was now a mere three weeks out.

So, like I always do in a moment of panic, I called my mom. It just goes to show, as grownup and independent as a girl can get, she still needs her mom every so often. My mom jumped right into action.

"Okay, here's what we'll do. I've got some really cool shelves I can bring up that will go perfectly in your dining room and then we can fill those up with little bites of food. We can set up a long table on the back patio for some more substantial bites, then we'll whip up some awesome drinks. We can decorate the tables with cool little baskets of fresh herbs and make it a farmer's market party."

Just like that. My mom threw these (full-sized) shelves into the back of her car, dropped the millions of things that she had going on, and drove the eight hours up to my house a couple of days later.

Meanwhile, I spent my free time calling all the local dives that Bill and I enjoyed most: the restaurant with the best chai, the one with the best cupcakes, and the one with the most attractive waitstaff. Just kidding, how inappropriate would that have been? I couldn't have my waiters looking better than me at my wedding party.

*Ingenious shelving idea with delicious treats.
You know you want one*

By some miracle (my mom), the party came together beautifully. We had delicious food, drinks, and dessert set up immaculately thanks to somebody's brilliant design vision (my mom). It was perfect and went off without a hitch.

Wait, back up. There was one small, pea-sized hitch. We were pregnant.

Before heading off to New Zealand, I made the authoritative decision to not refill my birth control pills. It's not that I wanted to have a honeymoon baby, it's just that the only time you really hear about people *trying* to get pregnant, is when they're having a hard time actually getting pregnant. So, I assumed that pulling the plug would mean that we'd find ourselves happily with child in a year or so. I know, maybe I should have paid closer attention in my sex ed classes instead of laughing along with the kid drawing penises in his notebook.

Apparently, we didn't anticipate how fertile we were together. Very fertile. That's why, a month after getting married, we found ourselves as soon-to-be-parents. I'll expound on that further. Right now, back to the wedding.

Only a small handful of people knew that I was barefoot and pregnant in my wedding dress on that sunny day. It felt so deliciously scandalous, but it actually wasn't at all. I had two wedding certificates to show for that.

My biggest curiosity with pregnancy symptoms was something called *pica*. It's a condition when pregnant mamas crave non-food items during pregnancy. Think grass clippings, laundry detergent, goose droppings…I was secretly excited to get pica and to relive that childhood memory of my parents swatting my hands away from my mouth as I eagerly tried to eat fistfuls of beads, dirt, and roly polies.

I was even more excited to get pica *during* our wedding party. How awesome would it be to attend a wedding where the bride suddenly stops halfway down the aisle for a snack of freshly mowed grass? That'd be an even funnier wedding that the ones where the bride and groom perform a choreographed dance to *Thriller*.

Alas, it didn't happen to me. The only thing that happened to me was that I couldn't fake a tan, or diet, or get my hair dyed like brides are apparently supposed to do before getting married. Which, when you think about it, those things are really no less bizarre than eating grass.

CHAPTER 20

Domestic Training isn't For the Weak of Stomach

I always assumed that I'd get married and have a family at some point in my life, since that's just what most people did, but it never occurred to me that I would have any sort of domestic responsibility in that family.

In the height of my aspiring-attorney days, I actually dreamed about marrying a man who was longing to stay at home with the kids while I worked full-time. If that didn't happen, I figured all those homemaker skills I'd need would sprout alongside my baby during pregnancy and once the kid was born, BAM, insta domestic goddess.

When I moved up to Boulder to be with Bill, I decided to open my own event planning business. I quit my job, then immediately asked the company if they were looking for a contract event planner to fill my spot. Turns out, they were. I loved what I did: the travel, the interactions, the buying of tchotchkes, the newly found party trick of being able to properly spell the word *tchotchkes*. I stayed busy with a handful of clients and got to work from home in my pajamas when I wanted to (which was always). I had found my professional niche.

But, as a new wife in a beautiful home, something inside of me started to itch. I knew that it was time to up my domestic game. I made sure I was sitting down when I broke the news to myself, for fear that I might faint from the shock. Quite the contrary, I actually found myself giddy at the possibilities that lay ahead of me, and imagined all these magnificent cakes and pastries I would soon be making. I wish I hadn't sat down for this news; I stood back up and did a little happy dance.

This was a big deal. *Domestic* was never a word that popped up on my anticipated life charts. I could count on one hand the times in my life I'd had any sort of urge to bake or sew something, and every time I acted on those urges, disaster struck.

Let's just say, if a blank space existed in my yearbook captioned "most likely to have her own cooking show," or "most likely to own a Michelin-rated restaurant," my picture would have been the last one chosen. Unless, of course, the subtitle to either of those was, "...where she unintentionally poisons people regularly." Then, I might be a candidate.

I'm not just being humble here, I'm sharing in full-disclosure to limit my liability in case you happen to come to my house and end up getting sick. You've been warned, I can no longer be held responsible.

In college, I couldn't even accomplish the simple task of soaking beans. For those of you with zero cooking savvy like myself, let me just tell you that soaking beans is about as easy as brushing your teeth. Only, instead of scrubbing back and forth with toothpaste, you put a bunch of beans in a big bowlful of water and let them sit overnight. I changed my mind, brushing your teeth is actually harder than soaking beans.

Instead of letting my beans sit in a bowlful of water however, I put them in a pot on the stove and proceeded to cook them (on a very low simmer, in my defense) for several hours on end. This is probably a good time to admit that following recipes is next to impossible for me.

Our apartment smelled like a herd of 100 sweaty triathletes had barged in, ran around the kitchen for a few laps, and then each pooped directly on the floor.

Needless to say, I was not the most popular among my roommates that week. I say "week" because it took at *least* that long for the smell to dissipate. Maybe longer. Plus, we had to throw that pot away, which as any poor college student can relate, meant that we would never buy a new one and would resort to cooking our food in a stove-top popcorn popper from that day forward. I was kindly asked not to participate in preparing roommate dinners anymore.

Going back further, I very rarely wanted to cook as a kid. I do remember one specific day however, when I was feeling especially optimistic to pass that childhood rite of passage of baking chocolate chip cookies without adult supervision.

Nobody knew yet that it was best to keep me far away from the kitchen, so when I called my mom at work to ask her for a recipe, she was excited about how grown up I was becoming.

She was also explicit that she was on her way to a meeting and only had a minute to chat. So, when she started rattling off the ingredients from memory, I jotted everything down using abbreviations.

I made a point to only abbreviate the *obvious* things so I wouldn't mix up something stupid. For example, "1 C S" clearly meant one cup sugar. It was like a fun little puzzle. I mean, when you stop to think about it, why do we use the full word for anything? It takes so much creative guesswork out of life.

"Excuse me," you'd ask at a touristy gift shop, "where's the R?"

"Oh, you mean the restaurant?" The salesperson would kindly respond.

"No, the other R," you'd shrug, amused.

"Oh, the rhinoceros exhibit?"

"That'd be the R.E., wouldn't it?"

"Then you must be talking about the 'Rent-a-Camel'" (I guess we're at the zoo in this example.)

"No," you'd say nervously while doing a little potty dance. "The *R*." And then you'd pee on the floor.

I'm not sure why I keep talking about going to the bathroom on the floor. I'm sorry, it's terribly vulgar of me. I'll stop now. The point I'm making is, as fun as it seems, *don't* abbreviate things. It could lead to someone urinating on your floor. In my case, it led to calling my mom back at work and asking her if we had any more baking soda.

"What in the world do you need more baking soda for?

There's a whole box in the pantry."

"Yeah, well I used it all for my cookies. They should really make those boxes bigger, you know?"

"You used it *all*?!"

"Yup. One cup."

"Do *NOT* put those cookies in the oven."

Too late. My cookies exploded all over the oven, setting off the fire alarm, and creating a couple of days' worth of cleaning for myself and anyone else who felt like helping. Nobody did. Thanks a lot, siblings.

Let me give you a bit of free advice and save you the hassle of cleaning your oven: if you see the abbreviation "1 C B.S." in a recipe, it's probably safe to assume that you're meant to use brown sugar instead of baking soda. You're welcome.

Amazingly, my mom still let me help out with dinner prep every so often. Only, instead of letting me stir the soup or anything oven-related, I was forever demoted to "cheese grater."

When Meghan and I lived together, I figured it was high past time to try my hand at cooking again. I wanted to develop at least some basic cooking skills so I could survive by bartering my chef services during the Zombie Apocalypse. I mean, as long as we aren't brain-munching Zombies ourselves, we'll all still have to eat regular food, right?

Meghan was a better chef than me, but something about working as a team brought her down to my level. You're only as strong as your weakest link, I guess. Even still, her cooking success gave me more confidence, so we set out with plans to make the best Christmas cookies known to man. How hard could it be?

Here's the thing with me and following recipes: I always (start out with the best intentions to) follow the directions, but Meghan and I were busy people and baking takes a long time and plus sometimes we didn't have the right ingredients and the closest store was (approximately 0.2) miles away. To top it all off, we had plenty of perfectly good food already at our house that would otherwise go to waste, so why wouldn't we just use that as part of the recipe?

We made a shopping trip specifically to pick up cookie ingredients, gingerbread-man sprinkles, and Christmas cookie cutters. (They were supposed to be stockings, but really looked more like those squatty crew socks that you can't even see peeking out from your sneakers.)

Not only were we going to make the world's best Christmas cookies, but we were going to make them dairy-free to accommodate Meghan's milk allergy. As a replacement for butter, we bought a tub of *Can't Believe it's Not Butter*, which I'm pretty sure says somewhere on the container that it's *not* meant for baking the world's best Christmas cookies. If it doesn't say that, there's a major case of false advertising going on there.

When we got home and pulled out all the ingredients, we realized that we were mysteriously out of vanilla. I mean, not a single drop in the little bottle. Where did it go? We never baked. Meghan neither confirmed nor denied a secret addiction to vanilla upon interrogation. Either way, we certainly weren't going to make an extra trip to the store just for vanilla, so we substituted some lime juice instead, because why not.

We mixed our cookie dough and couldn't believe how sticky it was. Our knee-jerk reaction was to add more flour. A lot more flour. Only after depleting our entire flour bag did we notice the fine print (okay, okay, it was the same size print as the rest of the recipe) saying that the dough was *supposed* to be sticky and needed to sit for an hour in the fridge to lose its stickiness. Oops. Oh well, adding all that flour saved us an hour of wait time, right?

The cookies actually came out of the oven looking pretty normal. Like little squatty gym-sock cookies. We were both too afraid to try them, though. So, we moved on to the next step: frosting them.

We followed the directions exactly (except for the lime juice in place of vanilla) and then tried it out. Now, I was once a child and have experienced my fair share of cotton candy, popsicles, and Halloween. But, I had never tasted anything so insanely sweet in my life as that frosting. I can't pinpoint what went wrong, but my best educated guess is that I mis-measured the sugar. Whoops.

Meghan took one lick and violently kicked the fridge because the sweet shot through her so hard. So, we did what any logical chef would do and we added peanut butter. I know, genius, right? Wrong. Let's just say that not even Milo would touch those morsels. We sent them off to the Island of Misfit Cookies, aka, the trash.

CHAPTER 21

Rhubarb Delight, Wherein "Delight" is a Highly Subjective Term

On one of our first dates, Bill made me dinner. Not like Kraft Mac & Cheese, but like a *real*, this took a couple of hours, dinner. Take note, guys, if you want to impress a girl, cook for her. Maybe even wear an apron. You won't regret the outcome.

There I was, not even able to make simple sugar cookies, and this guy was making me an incredible four-course meal. Score! I knew if I stuck with him, I wouldn't starve. (As anybody naturally does in an early dating relationship, I was very apt at making sure my basic hierarchy of needs were being met. Forget the nice jewelry and such, was he *feeding* me?)

Once we got more serious in our relationship, I made a deal with Bill: he could be the cook and I'd be the dishwasher. He was psyched and we shook on it without a moment's hesitation. Now that I'm thinking back on it, I'm a little offended how quickly he jumped on that deal. Someone must have tipped him off about my tendency to substitute lime juice for vanilla.

Then, something odd happened. As my heart grew more and more fond of Bill, I found myself actually wanting to *take care* of him. What was this new sensation I was feeling? Was I actually concerned with somebody else's well-being?

As hard as I tried, I couldn't shake the desire, so I started to (try to) cook for this man. I'm not sure that *my cooking* and *care-taking* should have been allowed in the same sentence, but Bill entertained and encouraged it. Although I think he was secretly a little bit sad that he wouldn't get the chance to wear his apron as much.

I'll get to my gardening skills next (another domestic Achilles' Heel of mine), but I'll foreshadow it by mentioning that my grandpa in Idaho, who is THE example when it comes to a green thumb, gifted us with a rhubarb plant. Does that statement sound as odd as I think it does?

Growing up, we loved visiting our grandparents for lots of reasons, but one of the reasons was to wander through my grandpa's garden. We especially loved tromping through the berry bushes (I'm sure my grandparents weren't quite as fond of the tromping.) We'd get our fill of raspberries, gooseberries, and rhubarb. I'm going to get a bit nostalgic for a second about each of these fruits, forgive me.

Raspberries: My grandma makes the world's best raspberry jam. Hands down. I'd put her up against your grandma in a jam contest any day.

Gooseberries: If you've never had one, go find one and

try it. Not because it will be this delicious little morsel that will make you wonder where it's been all your life, but because they are so blasted sour that I can't *believe* all of us little kids would eat them by the handful like candy. One year while we were there, we even took an old, splintery plank of wood (likely with rusty nails jutting out of it), leaned it against the side of a little hill in my grandparents' backyard and called it our playhouse. We'd sit underneath that plank for hours at a time. You were only allowed into the playhouse via the the secret password. My siblings and cousins might kick me out of the club for revealing the secret password—sorry guys, it's for the sake of the story. "Yrrebesoog." For those of you who need a little hand-holding now and then, that's "gooseberry" backwards. This is how obsessed we were with those little balls of face-puckering glory.

Rhubarb: I only recently learned that you are *not* supposed to eat rhubarb raw. Especially not the leaves because they're poisonous. But, of course, when you're a wild, foraging child living under a splintery plank of wood, those rules don't apply to you, so we'd pull rhubarb from my grandparents' garden right and left and suck on it like it was sugarcane. I'm not sure any of us ever attempted to eat the leaves so I can't entirely vouch for their poisonous nature, but just to play it safe, maybe stay away from them.

The point of my rambling is that there are a lot of fond memories of my grandpa's garden. So, as an adult, when I took Bill to Idaho for the first time, I gushed on and on about all the plants. My grandpa pulled up a handful of raspberry and rhubarb roots (he had since torn up the gooseberries. I guess not everybody finds them as delicious as we did) and handed them to us in a plastic grocery bag as we were leaving their house for the airport. My grandma also handed us a few jars of her ridiculously delicious raspberry jam.

At the airport, we braced ourselves knowing that we could likely get thrown into a one-sided mirror room and interrogated by the TSA about why we were traveling with plants. Instead, the plastic bag full of roots rode blissfully down the security conveyor belt, and our *jam* got stopped instead. Oh no, not my grandma's jam! Straight into the garbage can. I nearly cried. So, we boarded the airplane with our suitcases and a bunch of dirty plant stalks.

We planted the roots as soon as we got home. Or maybe it was several days after we got home…the details are a little hazy. The raspberries died right away and we thought the rhubarb had, too. But lo and behold, half a year later, little baby rhubarb started popping out of the ground. It was a Christmas miracle in the middle of May!

My urge to play caretaker took over, and I decided to bake a rhubarb tart. I found a recipe that looked easy enough, then read and reread the directions to make absolutely certain that this tart would be a success. I tightened my apron strings and got to work.

Bill came home that evening to find what looked like an incredible egg and bacon quiche. He was semi-impressed and also a little bit curious as to why I put whole strips of bacon in my quiche instead of cutting them up a bit. I told him it was not actually an egg and bacon quiche and that those big strips of "bacon" were actually big strips of rhubarb. *Semi-impressed* turned into *semi-disgusted*, but also entirely amused. I'm pretty certain he keeps me around for entertainment purposes.

What led to such a debacle, you ask? How could someone possibly mess up something as simple as a rhubarb tart? I have a perfectly logical explanation. As I mentioned, I read and reread the directions, but kept getting caught on the wording: "Cut rhubarb into lengths and arrange in circles in the pan." Totally confusing, right? I spent way too much time thinking really hard about what that could possibly mean, and the only thing that kept coming to mind was the conversation I would have with my hair stylist when I went in for a haircut. It usually sounded something like this:

"Could you cut my hair in layers, please?"

"What kind of layers?"

"Oh, you know, varying lengths and such."

"Gotcha. Would you care for another head massage?"

"Ooh, yes please."

By this logic, I figured the recipe must have meant to cut my rhubarb into *varying* lengths. I did my best; some pieces were an inch long, others were up to six inches long, and everything in between. I had to give myself credit; there were a lot of lengths going on with my rhubarb. Then, as I was instructed to do, I circled it around the tart pan. The six inch pieces were a little bit tricky to circle around since they were just about the same size as the pan, but I smashed them in anyway. Then, I threw that tart into the oven, prematurely proud of my accomplishment.

When the timer went off, I dutifully stuck a toothpick into the center of my masterpiece. The eggs hadn't even *started* to cook. What?! I figured it was either because six inches was a couple inches too long to cut my rhubarb lengths, or it was because we were at high altitude. I gave myself the benefit of the doubt, went with the second theory and threw the tart back in the oven at a slightly higher heat, because that helps it cook faster, right?

I served up the tart, trying to mask the fact that the "custard" was somehow burned on the top, but not at all cooked in the middle. Bill poked at it with his fork as though it was alive and held up a limp rhubarb stalk. "What went wrong," he asked so sweetly while choking down his raw eggs. I'm not sure if raw eggs or raw rhubarb is worse for you, but I'm guessing you should just stay away from both of them. In a true act of irony, I was poisoning the man I wanted so badly to take care of.

"I have *no* idea. I followed the recipe exactly." Deflated, I pulled the cookbook out to show him. He quickly noticed and pointed out something right at the very top of the list of ingredients. It said, "One pound of rhubarb - cut into roughly one inch lengths." Ooooh. That made the directions further down a lot more clear. How did I *miss* that?

On the plus side, Milo really liked my rhubarb tart, so at least I had that going for me.

My ~~bacon and egg quiche~~ rhubarb pie, complete with "lengths" of rhubarb. I took creative liberty in choosing to add almond slices

CHAPTER 22

Don't Be Afraid to Get Your Hands Dirty

Terrible rhubarb tart aside, I was so thrilled that something was actually *growing* in my yard, that I decided to start an ENTIRE garden. I'm sure you can guess it, but I had never gardened in my life. My closest experience to gardening was when my dad (who inherited my grandpa's green thumb) would spend his Saturday mornings working in his garden, and I'd run out with my little toys to play in the dirt.

One Saturday, I buried a little plastic figurine collie dog, ran off for a minute, and came back to retrieve my toy. No luck. I could not find that dumb little dog anywhere. I spent hours looking that day, the next day, and for weeks and even months after that. Sigh, it was terribly traumatic. To this day, I could tell you *exactly* what that little plastic toy looked like, smelled like, and even tasted like. That experience ruined me from gardening, which really isn't fair because it wasn't actually *gardening's* fault that I lost my little collie dog.

Putting my traumatic past behind me, I dedicated a small plot of our backyard to be my garden spot. I followed Bill's suggestion to start simple and blocked off a three-foot square. In that tiny square, I ambitiously intended to grow tomatoes, peppers, and squash. I marked each of their designated corners with a wooden spoon. If you're nodding your head and smiling right now because of how perfectly laid out my garden sounds, I would *not* recommend counting on your garden to provide self-sufficient food supply.

I didn't realize that within days, my viney little veggie starters would overtake my small garden and crowd into each other's designated spaces. It was pure disaster. Didn't they know they were supposed to stay behind their wooden spoon borders? Seriously.

Just as I started giving up hope (this is a lie, I had given up hope long before), I saw something in my garden! Two teensy, tiny, little tomatoes. When I say teensy, tiny, I really mean it. These tomatoes were about the size of a Gobstopper. It was a miracle.

Even more miraculous was the fact that those weren't the only thing in my garden. There also happened to be a miniature red pepper about the size of a dime and a little, tiny jalapeño about the size of a caterpillar who had just eaten a big meal.

Four things grew in my garden! Four minuscule little vegetables grew in my tiny, itty bitty, little garden. The only explanation I have is that each plant must have seen how downtrodden I was when they started to crowd the garden, and agreed to respect each other's space and grow just a little bit. I don't know.

What I *do* know is that we had a delicious tiny bite of itty bitty vegetable salad for dinner that night. And boy, did it taste like victory to me.

My veggies in comparison to a normal-sized apple. Adorbs, no?

CHAPTER 23

Sew Like the Wind, and Other Poetic, yet Failed, Attempts

With baking and gardening well underway, I figured what the hell, I may as well try my hand at sewing while I was at it. I had never wanted to learn how to sew until I got pregnant and made the big mistake of looking at baby clothes.

Baby clothes are dangerous because they're just big clothes shrunk down to miniature sizes, and it's just a basic fact that if you take anything at all and make a smaller version of it, it will be ridiculously adorable. Except for raccoons. Raccoons are never adorable.

Don't even get me started on baby shoes. I was toast. The weird thing is, even though baby clothes are smaller than adult clothes, they actually cost *more*. By all accounts, it doesn't make sense. I knew that if I didn't find a solution to my newly-found obsession, my bank account would also be toast.

Enter my brilliant idea to *sew* all these bite-size outfits instead of buying them. I mean, fabric and thread cost next to nothing, right? (I didn't actually know because I had never purchased anything like that.) But, how hard could it be? All I needed was a sewing machine and in no time flat, I'd not only create an entire wardrobe for my baby, but I'd also clothe all the babies in Ethiopia.

Let me be more truthful. Sewing was not an *entirely* foreign art to me. When I was little, my grandma (the same one who makes amazing raspberry jam) would bring me little cross-stitch projects whenever she visited (usually cat-related to keep me interested). One time, we even sewed a cat pillow together. By that, I obviously mean that she did all the sewing and I sat next to her, distracted with my stuffed animals and occasionally asking her when my pillow was going to be finished.

Slightly more impressive, I also made a quilt once. I know, right? I've repressed most of those memories, but I do recall it was for a service project. As I sat scowling on the couch, pushing the needle in and out of my quilt with my raw fingers over and over again to make the ties, my parents stood, mouths agape, taking pictures of me because they couldn't believe what was actually happening. That pain on my face was real, people. Thanks for the encouragement, Mom and Dad.

Since my point in learning to sew was to save money, I proudly bought the cheapest used sewing machine I could find online. When you're a budding master sewer, you don't need to do research or check reviews on the machine you're going to use; you'll sew masterpieces on anything.

I changed my tune after spending three solid days trying to get that complete piece of junk to work properly. Three. Solid. Days. I took that lousy little sewing machine to a sew and vac shop. I would like to know who in the history of the world decided that sewing machines and vacuums must always go together and that a "sew" can not exist without a "vac" in any shop title. The store I wandered into was especially awesome, mostly because every inch of it was covered in carpet, from the floors to the walls to the countertop. I felt slightly claustrophobic and a little bit allergic. This was not my first time in that shop. A few months prior, Bill and I went vacuum shopping like the newlyweds we were and had the most *fantastic* experience I think you could ever expect from such an outing. It looked a little something like this:

Bill: "We're here to buy a vacuum"

Vacuum shop guy: "We have those."

B: "Cool."

VSG: "This one you're looking at is our best seller. It's on sale from $300 to $250."

B: "Great, we'll take it." (Thanks to Bill, we had already done our research online. I don't believe in that sort of thing; buying blindly is so much more *interesting*.)

VSG: "If you want something slightly nicer, they do go up in cost and features from there. This one has a rubber handle. But it's $500. $400 dollars."

B: "Wha?"

VSG: "$500 normally, but $400 on sale."

B: "So, what exactly is this sale? Like 25% off or something?"

VSG: "No. This one's not on sale, but I feel like giving it to you for $400."

B: "Okay thanks. But, I don't think it's worth an extra $150 just for a rubber handle."

VSG: "Then I'll give it to you for $300 since you called before you came in."

B: "You've got yourself a deal!"

VSG: "Can I help you build it?"

B: "That'd be great, thanks!"

At that point, Vacuum Shop Guy pulled out the box, stuck the fancy rubber handle into the rest of the vacuum and viola, it was built. I'm really glad we got help with that.

B: "How about vacuum bags? What are the best ones?"

VSG: "Well these are the highest rated vacuum bags around."

B: "…and what does that mean exactly?"

VSG: "It means that no other bags are rated higher."

Then we talked a little bit more about the vacuum's features. Vacuum Shop Guy was very eager to whisper some *secret tips-of-the-trade features* that you couldn't hear about otherwise; except that those same features were highlighted in a big, bold font on the homepage of the vacuum website. See what you get for doing your research?

I asked him why they always sold vacuums and sewing machines together and he said, "Ya know, I've worked in the business for 30 years and I have no idea. We are looking to get some ceiling fans in here to sell, too. And some tasers." And I knew that he was serious.

On our way out the door, he threw in two extra vacuum belts. "One to use and one to lose," he said.

Based on that experience, there was no question that I'd return there for my sewing needs. I hoped that maybe he would have gotten the tasers in by then, but you can't get too excited about those types of things.

I took my machine in, set it on the carpet counter, and Vacuum Shop Guy immediately said, not softening the blow at all, "You wasted your money. This piece of crap will never work right, and I'm not gonna waste my time trying to fix it for ya."

"Oh." I was a little unsure what else to say.

He wasn't done, though. "Sewing machines just aren't made like they used ta be. They're all crap. Now, I got this one here that'll last you hundreds of years and you can do anything to it. You can throw it on the ground and jump on it if you want and it'll still sew like new. It's for $589 but I'll give it to you for $210 because of the poor economy…"

He then went off for several minutes about how he's been trying to get his competitor's information out of the yellow pages. Then he started vacuuming his counter while talking on the phone with his granddaughter about how school was.

Once I got his attention again, I agreed to his "poor economy" rate and $210 later, I was the proud owner of an apparently accident-proof sewing machine. I won't lie, it did hurt a little bit to think that that $210 could have paid for one pair of already-made baby shoes.

I figured that a good place to start sewing would be with baby blankets since they weren't too complicated and didn't require much sewing. I knew I'd master those immediately and could then quickly move on to something more challenging. The (first) problem came when I realized I couldn't hold my hands still to save my life. How are you supposed to sew in a straight line?! Impossible. And keeping your fabric flat so there aren't a bunch of pockets and scrunched areas? Forget about it.

The real mind-boggling part for me though, were the

corners. How in the *world* do people fold those blanket corners so perfectly? It made no sense. And since following directions, as you've gathered by now, is not my forte, I couldn't trust a YouTube video or anything else to help me figure it out. I'd just have to muster through it myself.

That's why my first baby blanket took me about three times as long as it should have, and was more the shape of a trapezoid than a rectangle. Let's not even mention the corners. They looked like little pigs-in-a-blanket hanging off each side of my geometric blanket.

To top it all off, upon inspection, Bill pointed out that I had somehow sewed a couple of pins *into* the blanket. My poor baby.

With my first project behind me (I told myself it was a success in order to keep my momentum strong), I moved on to a pair of baby yoga pants just in case my baby came out dying to do a bit of stretching. I mean, that womb's gotta get cramped, right?

Halfway through my pants project, Bill very gently noted to me, "You better hope the baby gets your dad's long legs…"

I held up the little pants to try to argue my side, but couldn't deny that the extremely long and flared legs of my little pants would probably be too big even for a four-year old. The one thing I *could* hold on to though, was that the waistline seemed to be a perfect fit for a newborn. And that's when I realized that I had sewn the back of the pants to the front of the pants.

By now, my stubbornness had set in and I just HAD to conquer this sewing thing! I picked my confidence up off the floor to try another pair of little yoga pants. And, guess what? That second pair of yoga pants actually ended up looking (and functioning) like pants. One for the win!

With my confidence back in check (maybe *slightly* more than it should have been given my track record), I knew my next move was to follow an actual pattern. I picked out a cute little dress pattern that I could have *sworn* said "easy" somewhere on it. It was not easy.

There should be a college linguistics course for sewing since reading those patterns seems like a foreign language. I'm sure all of you pro sewers will roll your eyes at me, but seriously, how am I supposed to translate this:

"Turn back edge to INSIDE along outer fold line, forming interfacing; press. Baste close to inner edge." It's all Greek to me.

The only thing I knew clearly after reading and rereading those directions was that I needed to throw them away. I mean, I had already cut out all the proper pieces and had the picture of what the dress was supposed to look like. What more did I actually need?

I know you're waiting to hear about another failed attempt at sewing, but first of all, that's just mean of you, and second of all, my finished product actually looked like a dress! So there. Granted, there were a few extra pieces of cut fabric that I had *no* idea where to put, but there were no pins poking out or anything. A clear win. That is, until I actually had a baby to put in the dress. Only then, when Bill pointed out that my baby's arm was turning blue because the dress sleeve was cutting off her circulation, did I realize that maybe sewing wasn't quite as easy as I initially had thought.

CHAPTER 24

Forget the Textbooks, Self Discovery is Your Best Tool

You're mildly amused, but wondering why I'm sharing all of these awesomely tragic and self-demoralizing failed attempts, right? To prove that owning your own strong requires two simple words: Keep trying.

If you find yourself excited about something, don't ignore that. I guarantee the average person is *un*interested in way more things than he or she is actually interested in, so when you discover something that intrigues you, hang on to it.

Did I suck at all things domestic? Absolutely. Do I still suck at all things domestic? I can proudly and honestly say that I do not. In fact, I'm known in my circle of friends as *the chef, the sewer,* AND *the gardener.* So there.

Can I follow a recipe now? No, not really. Can I translate a sewing pattern? Definitely not. Do I just randomly scatter seeds around in my garden and see what pops up? Yes. So how, you ask, can you claim to be good at any of those things? Because I've learned a lot of things about myself along the way and found my own approaches that work *for me*. For example, I've accepted that I cannot follow directions to save my life. So, I don't. I experiment, and I hack, and I practice a lot because I love it. I don't fit in a mold. I never have and I never will. Neither will you.

I was still working as an event planner, but the more I delved into this new world of *homemade*, the more I started to realize that maybe it wasn't going to be my career that defined me in life. I felt strong when I worked with my hands, fulfilled when I finished a project, and complete when I shared my passion with my friends and family.

That definition of a Pisces I once used to mock now felt a little cozier when I tried it on for size: creative, kind, sensitive…those words didn't sound so weak to me anymore. They sounded *true*.

It was time to fully accept my stars. It was time to admit that yes, I was a passive aggressive, type-B personality who was anything but detail-oriented (sorry for lying on my resume about that one, all prospective employers), and who doesn't like confrontation.

Psychiatrists say we can know our true selves by thinking back to what we were like as children. I'm actually not sure if any psychiatrists do say this, but I think it's true and it just sounds more legitimate if it's backed by psychiatrists, so let's pretend.

I thought back to how badly I wanted to take care of animals in a veterinarian clinic. I was born to be a caregiver and a lover, not a kickass feminist.

With that discovery under my belt, it was time to try something else completely new: growing a baby.

CHAPTER 25

Growing Babies and Other Normal Abnormalities

I was not the first woman in the world to ever get pregnant—thanks for stealing that thunder, Eve—nor would I be the last. But, when *you're* the one who's pregnant, it feels so magical and special that you can't fathom how it could possibly be an everyday thing that millions of others have experienced, too. When *you're* pregnant, you feel like the entire world will stop to watch you pass, to make sure you're comfortable, to help you blow your nose. You feel like the entire axis of the universe has shifted to revolve around you instead of around the Sun. You feel like a freaking goddess.

I knew I was pregnant weeks before taking the test. I also knew I was probably just imagining it all, so I didn't mention anything to Bill until the day I was supposed to have my period. Our days went about as usual, only I couldn't concentrate on a single thing because I kept waiting for my period to not start.

Eventually, I gave up trying to get any work done and headed to our little local convenience store to buy a pregnancy test. Of course, the worker on shift that day was a perfect Johnny Depp (*Chocolat* era) look-alike. Take my word for it, buying a pregnancy test from Johnny Depp is a bit nerve-racking. This guy didn't help the situation much, either. He studied that little box intensely before handing it back to me saying, "Whelp, have a fun night!"

I rushed home, eager to make a romantic dinner and share the possible news. I didn't make it to the romantic dinner part, though. Instead, the second I stepped in the door, I couldn't hold it in and found the words just spilling out. "I'm pregnant." Bill started laughing. I couldn't be mad given the fact that I laughed when he proposed. Reason #876 why we're compatible, I suppose. After he collected himself, the questions started:

"How do you know?" He grinned.

"I don't, I just have a hunch."

"When was your period supposed to be?"

"Today…I think."

He rolled his eyes. "You think? Plus, aren't you supposed to wait a few days after? What if it's just late? The day's not even over yet!"

"Like I said, I just have a hunch. You shouldn't question a woman's hunch, you know."

"Okay fine, let's get a pregnancy test, then."

"I already got one."

"Wow, you're serious about this."

As comfortable as we were together, Bill and I hadn't scaled the *peeing in front of each other* phase in our relationship. In an effort to be a part of it all, he unwrapped the pregnancy test and slid it under the bathroom door to me. But, even with the door separating us, I found myself with a severe case of performance anxiety. After a few minutes and only a drop or two that most definitely missed the stick, I came out of the bathroom deflated and put the stick on the counter knowing I had lost this round.

I started chugging as much water as I could handle to prepare myself to try again when Bill mustered, "Uh, are you *sure* you didn't get anything on the stick?" I made my way cautiously to the counter where a bright, pink plus sign stared up at us.

"That's gotta be wrong," I gasped, suddenly convinced that there was no way in a million years I could be pregnant. "I mean, maybe we let it sit too long or something. We should get another one just to make sure."

I have to believe that no woman since the beginning of plastic pregnancy test history has been satisfied with taking just one pregnancy test once they see that affirmation. Here I was, completely certain for the last month that I was pregnant, and then in a split second, I couldn't believe my eyes.

We started the jaunt back down to the convenience store to pick up another test. Of course, Johnny Depp was still working the counter.

"I can't go back in there," I insisted. "You have to buy it."

Bill puffed up his chest with manly courage and stepped confidently through the doors. I watched from a safe distance as Bill and Johnny bantered for a few minutes before Bill came practically skipping out of the store.

"What were you guys talking about?" I tried to sound nonchalant.

"Oh, not much," Bill shrugged, "He told me this was the second pregnancy test he had sold today. I laughed and said, 'Yeah, the first was my girlfriend.' Then he said, 'Oh man, I've been there before. Good luck!'"

"Wait, you called me your *girlfriend*?!" I started to laugh. "This is a pretty serious time to use the term wife, or you could have even pulled out fiancé, but *girlfriend??* Wow, you must be really nervous about this…"

Bill's face lost all its color. "I didn't even realize I did that! I was wondering why he was eyeing my wedding band when he made his comment. He must have been empathizing!"

We had apparently uncovered the sad truth that the Johnny-Depp-Look-Alike was a floozy. Oh well, we had bigger fish to fry that night.

Back at home, my *boyfriend* handed me the second test under the bathroom door. I aimed really hard this time and was proud of my accuracy. We set the timer to check the stick the second we were supposed to, and sure enough, another plus sign smiled back at us.

And, here's the thing with probably any situation that surprises you, good or bad: there was no swelling music, no misty eyes, no lifting me up and twirling me around. Instead, we stared at the test in shock for a good minute or so, then congratulated each other with a calm, contented hug and a quiet, "Whelp, here we go!"

CHAPTER 26

Talents Can Sometimes Stumble Right into You

I had always assumed that at some point in my life, I'd get pregnant. The thing I didn't anticipate though, was how damn *good* I'd be at it. I mean that in the humblest way possible, of course. I just had no idea I would rock pregnancy the way I rocked pregnancy.

Here I'd spent my entire life making to-do lists and intellectually trying to figure out who/what/where/when/why about every aspect of life and then *BAM*, I get knocked up and my body takes over my intellect and just, you know, GROWS A FREAKING BABY.

I first realized how awesome I was at growing a baby when I hit my six-week pregnancy mark. Like any expectant mother who can't help herself and reads *way* too many articles and forums about pregnancy, I knew that week six was when all the yucky symptoms started.

I waited. I watched the seconds tick down until week six officially started, dreading every moment of it. But then, something miraculous happened. Nothing. I woke up feeling completely fine. Not even an ounce of nausea. I felt completely, and uncomfortably *normal*.

I'm hesitant to say that because I know more mamas than not feel much more than *nothing* in their early pregnancies. I'm probably getting all sorts of hate glares right now, but does it make it better if I sincerely say that I continually wish my good pregnancy fortune on any pregnant woman I see?

The sad truth is, I actually felt a little bit disappointed. It was similar to the disappointment you'd feel if you were preparing for the holidays with all of the anticipation and anxiety that goes with it, and then Christmas morning comes and goes without anyone even acknowledging what day it is let alone stacking presents in front of you. Of course, presents and vomiting are two fairly different things, but I still felt oddly gypped.

So of course, I panicked. Something must be wrong! I jumped out of bed and ran straight to my computer to do some legitimate research. Hundreds of (hardly legitimate) forums popped up with thousands of women worried about the same thing, assuring each other that this was just as *normal* as puking, and to stop worrying about it and to go enjoy their pregnancy free of symptoms. Oh, and by the way, what the hell is wrong with you?!

They were right to question. What *was* wrong with me? Here I was, lucky to not be laying in a pool of my own vomit, and yet I was worried about it. I was being ridiculous and decided then and there that I would take the advice of those forum writers, and enjoy feeling well instead of worrying myself sick over not being sick. That should be a country song title. Whoever uses it, you can send a percentage of your royalties directly to my house, thanks.

In an effort to celebrate my health, I started practicing prenatal yoga, which felt inwardly wonderful and outwardly *too hippie* at the same time. I sat in the classes, loving every second of it, but I wore a stern face when I emerged from the studio, just to prove that I was *not* a floaty, metaphysical yoga girl.

Then, one day out of the blue as I was just sitting and enjoying being pregnant, something became very, *very* clear to me. *This* is what I was meant to be doing! For the first time in my life, I knew without a doubt that I was doing exactly what was right for me. I was on this earth to be a vessel for this baby and to mother this child. Never in a million years would I have written that down on one of my to-do lists. Strong women don't live their lives to have and raise children, right? But, I felt more comfortable and confident in my own skin during pregnancy than I had ever before. I felt alive and vibrant, purposeful, and—get this—*strong*.

The really awesome thing was, it had nothing to do with what was going on inside of my head. This pregnancy was happening entirely in my body because I had no *idea* how to build a baby. With my sense of following directions, I'm sure the babe would have come out with its arm attached to its forehead or something if it were up to my intellect. But, it wasn't. It was up to my body, and somehow, my body knew *exactly what to do*.

I realized for the thousandth time in my life, that maybe my definition of a *strong woman* was still a little bit narrow-minded.

CHAPTER 27

Stings, Bites, and other
Unfortunate Consequences of Pregnancy

Even though I mostly did a good job loving my symptom-free pregnancy, I might have become a little too self-confident, because the Universe decided to teach me a little lesson.

It's said that pregnant women are a favorite of mosquitos. First, because pregnant women produce more blood and second, because they're bigger targets. I made up the second fact, but let's face it, it's true. I happened to be walking proof of this theory. Bugs of all shapes and sizes wouldn't leave me alone. It made me realize just how Scarlett Johansson might feel walking into a bar full of drunken sickos who love boobs—It is not fun.

The bug bites alone were pretty brutal. Then one day, I stepped on a bee. For any Buddhists out there, I'm pretty sure it was his fault and not mine, so hopefully karma is on my side with that one. It was my first bee sting *ever*. I'm not entirely sure how I had lived my entire life to that point without falling victim to a bee. It felt like a superpower of some sort.

Thanks to a quick thinking husband, I was quickly escorted to the ~~emergency~~ family room and set up on ~~a hospital bed~~ our couch. Lots of baking soda, ice, tea bags, and chocolate ice cream later, I was pronounced *healed*.

Life went back to normal until the next morning when I woke up with a foot the size of Rhode Island. Did I mention it was also covered in pustulous blisters? You're welcome for the visual. After a not-so-silent freak-out, I called my OB to freak out some more. "I'm allergic to bees! I didn't even know it, but I've got to be. You should see my foot!"

The automated message system wasn't interested in my story, and instead urged me to press "0" for reception or "2" para hablar en español.

When I finally got in touch with a doctor, she listened to my situation and then audibly rolled her eyes. I'm pretty sure I heard her cover the phone's mouthpiece with her hand and whisper to her coworkers, "Paranoid first time mom…"

She came back on and assured me that the baby would not die if I soaked my foot in Epsom Salt. And then she kindly invited me to call a regular doctor next time something non-baby related happened.

A full week later, my foot didn't look any different. Let me repeat that in case you fell asleep for a second. A FULL WEEK later. I had become a monster. I prayed that my baby would still love me even with a grilled turkey leg for a foot.

Just as the reaction finally started to dissipate, get this,

I GOT STUNG BY A SECOND BEE. I'm not entirely sure that one wasn't my fault. Sorry Buddhists.

The blisters and swelling came right back. Only this time, one of the blisters broke, giving me a secondary infection that laid me out flat for a handful of days. I really wanted to call my OB again just to make sure there was no chance that my child would be born with a stinger, but I resisted the urge.

Later that same month, bee stings behind me, we ventured up to a cabin in the mountains for a little family reunion. Per usual, I was the crème de la crème for all the mosquitos, but what I didn't expect was to wake up at 3 a.m. to see something flying around our room. It took me a couple of minutes to realize that it was a bat.

I woke Bill up, and bless his heart, he didn't panic the way I likely would have if somebody was shaking me violently in my sleep, and frantically whispering, "…it's flying all over the place…it's pretty big…they're such nasty looking little critters…"

We opened the window in an effort to free the thing, but it didn't want to leave and chose instead to perch itself in the corner right above our bed. Then we did what any sensible person would do in the middle of the night and fell back asleep.

When we woke up the next morning, our new little pet was still happily snoozing in the corner. I actually can't say for sure that it was happy because if you've ever had a close up look at a bat, you'll understand that it's impossible to focus on things like bat-smiles when the only thing that really catches your attention is how odd their little arms and claws look attached to their wings. It's just creepy.

We ran into the kitchen where everyone else was already eating breakfast and told them about our new friend. All the kids squealed and followed us back to our room to see the flying rodent.

"Guess what else?" Bill started in on some improvisation. "It bit Chelsea right on the neck!" He moved my hair aside to reveal a giant red bump on the base of my neck. I hadn't noticed the bite before and was just as shocked as the kids were. But, instead of joining in the choir of screams like I wanted to do, I kept my cool. You'd be proud.

We chased the bat around for a bit, and finally caught it in a fishing net. The only thing creepier than those little bat arms and claws is seeing a bat run down a wall. I'm pretty sure I'll be up with nightmares about that tonight. Then, we set it free to scare the poop out of somebody else.

A couple of days later, on our drive back to Boulder, Bill's sister called to chat. Bill told her about our funny story of sleeping with a bat in our room, but she didn't find it the least bit humorous.

"You have to go to the doctor right away," she pleaded. "That bat may have given you rabies."

She went on to say that two separate sets of her friends also woke up with bats flying around their rooms and they were both strongly advised to get rabies shots. Apparently bats can land on things with feather-like skill, so if you're asleep, you won't feel one on you. Also, their fangs are so small that you likely wouldn't notice a bite.

What an over-dramatic response! Don't take our funny story away from us. Geez. My curiosity got the better of me because Bill's sister isn't one to fudge her facts, so I started researching on my phone. Here's what I learned:

i. Rabies is 100% fatal in people.
ii. There's no way to know for sure if you really have rabies or not until you start showing symptoms. But, by that point, it's too late—you're a goner.
iii. Most rabies cases in the US come from bat bites.
iv. You can tell if a bat has rabies if it's acting unusual, like flying into people's houses and not leaving when it's shooed away.
v. Rabies is 100% fatal. Did I mention that one already?

We were already two days past the incident. Who knew how much longer we had before the symptoms started showing? Time was of the greatest essence. "We need to get rabies shots NOW!" I grabbed the wheel of the car and squealed us straight to the closest emergency room. Just kidding, I didn't. Instead, I probably started rocking back and forth chanting "I'm too young to die."

But, of course, there was one tiny problem: I was growing a baby. Were rabies shots safe for a pregnant lady? I argued with myself if this situation counted as "baby related" or not, but finally hit my OB's number in the speed dial. Maybe I'd become known as "*that* lady," but it was better than dying.

The poor receptionist who answered the phone was part of this conversation:

"IthinkimighthavegottenbitbyaBATandineedRABIESshots.isthatsafeformybaby?"

"Excuse me?"

"Bat. Rabies shots. Safe?" I said it just like a frantic caveman.

"Um…"

"Oh yeah, I'm pregnant…and might have rabies."

Complete silence for way more time than I felt like I could afford.

"I'm going to have someone call you back in a few minutes."

Ten precious minutes later, the doctor called me back to let me know that she had called an all-office emergency meeting on my account to determine whether or not rabies shots were safe during pregnancy. Here was their conclusion:

"We think you should get the shots. There's no real proof showing if they're safe or not because what pregnant woman would willingly be a part of that study? But, we figure if you *do* have rabies, you're going to die and that's not very good for the baby, either."

I could appreciate their logic. We drove straight to the emergency room and each received SIX shots. Then, we had to promise to come back once a week for the next two months for two more shots each visit.

On the one hand it sucked, but on the other hand, it kind-of made me want to book a trip to live on a bat rescue in a developing country because I was now immune to bats. Check me out, a new superpower!

I was truly relieved that at our 20-week ultrasound, our baby did not appear to have a stinger or creepy arm-wings.

That little black thing is the bat. Because, yes, we had the wherewithal to take a picture of it...

CHAPTER 28

Oh Boy, Oh Boy, Oh Girl

Bill and I went back and forth about whether or not we wanted to find out the gender of our baby before it was born. Bill was in the "let's be surprised at the birth" camp, while I sided with the campers who ask, "isn't pushing a baby out of your vagina surprise enough for one day?"

So, we painted a compromise: I would bring a little note card to the ultrasound visit on which the tech could write the gender and seal it for us. Then, we could decide if and when we wanted to open the card.

Just for the record, I made the card from scratch. I know, impressive, right? Because folding a piece of cardstock in half and sticking it in an envelope was no small task. That's how awesome my domestic skills had gotten by that point.

Bill and I both *knew* this baby was a girl. It's funny when people say that because of course, everyone just *knows* any baby's gender...50% of the time. When somebody calls it right, they gloat and brag about how intuitive they are and bring it up whenever they can for the rest of their lives. When somebody calls it wrong, they sink into oblivion, never to be asked for their opinion again.

Even though I *knew*, I wanted to really know, just in case the baby was actually a boy. I mean, I'm all about this rising trend in people deciding that they were born the wrong gender and publicly switching it up, but I didn't want to be the core reason for my son to have a gender identity crisis.

"…it all started in the womb when my mom would talk to me through her belly and call me a *she*," he'd gush on during his interview with Diane Sawyer. "I have vague recollections of being put into a nursery covered in pink. It's my favorite color to this day."

Our ultrasound appointment was going great, until the tech asked us the million dollar question, "Do you want to know what you're having?"

I panicked, "You mean we aren't having a human baby? It's a bat after all, isn't it?"

When I realized what she actually meant, my mind went blank. What had we decided? Did we want to find out? I looked to Bill for guidance, but his face was just as confused as mine. The ultrasound tech was not amused by our sudden amnesia. She tapped her foot impatiently as we fumbled around blankly for our answer.

Finally, my sharp husband came to, "Wait, didn't you bring that card?" Ah yes! The little homemade card I labored hours over (it's harder than you think to fold a straight line).

The impatient foot tapping continued while I dug

around the depths of my purse in hot pursuit of the notecard. Why does everything take longer when somebody is waiting on you?

A few hours later, I found the card and passed it over to the doctor, gushing about how I made it and isn't that special, and…the tech couldn't care less. She snatched the paper out of my hand and quickly scribbled something inside, sealed the envelope, and handed it back to me. My overly-dramatic pregnancy emotions went from feeling hurt that she didn't want to know the backstory of the card, to offended that she didn't compliment me on the awesomeness of my craftiness, to mad that there was no pomp and circumstance included while she wrote. I'm not sure what I was expecting, maybe little fireworks shooting out of the pen—you know, something simple.

Soon enough, the card was back in my palm where it immediately starting burning a hole. There was no way I could keep it sealed for more than a few seconds. Bill saw my twitching hands and snatched the card away from me; putting it back in the black hole of my purse, possibly never to be found again. On the car ride home, I anxiously tapped my fingers on the dashboard and asked every few seconds if he was ready to open it yet.

I'm not sure how he stayed so calm, but he easily kept changing the subject and acting as though a really exciting bit of news wasn't resting in my purse. I finally convinced myself that maybe it *was* best to wait until we got home to open it so that Bill didn't get too excited with the announcement and accidentally drive into oncoming traffic. For safety's sake, we'd open the card the second we got home.

Bill had different plans, though. He parked the car and announced, "I'm going to go take a nap." Bill comes from a long line of nappers and takes his rest time very seriously. I knew he couldn't be swayed.

I tried to occupy myself with something, *anything*, but found myself sitting and staring at my purse. This must be what torture felt like. Unless, of course, you lived anywhere other than a first-world country without food or a house, or are a POW. Then, it just felt like lazily sitting on a comfy couch and whining.

After an hour or so of lazy whining, I heard Bill rustling around. He was awake! Not long after, I heard mumbling alongside the rustling. I peeked in the bedroom and saw that he was now on the phone, and it didn't sound like it was going to be a short conversation. Harrumph!

Another hour passed before I heard him conclude the call. I could hardly contain myself and started racing up the stairs like a clumsy retriever puppy whose feet are too big for his body. But, before I made it to the landing, there was a knock at our front door. Seriously, Universe? Seriously?

When I opened the door, three guys came traipsing in asking for Bill. I recognized one of them as the chatty electrician Bill had been working with on our house lighting. I had yet another sinking suspicion that this would not be a short conversation.

The second their interaction ended, I escorted the guys back to the front door where, lo and behold, Meghan and her husband were standing on the front porch. I had completely forgotten that I invited them over for dinner thinking that we would share our baby-gender news with them over chips and salsa. Instead, a sealed envelope still taunted me from the countertop, teasing me with the thought that at this rate, we really wouldn't know our baby's gender until it was born.

Once the house finally cleared and the moon had fully replaced the sun in the sky, Bill sat back and sighed, "I'm so tired. Maybe we should wait until tomorrow to open the card." I'll never know if he was kidding or not, but I did not take it as a joke. I (not so) calmly explained that I might just *die* if we didn't open that card NOW!

Bill watched my dramatics, smiled, then took me by my hand and led me out to the front porch swing—the same swing we got engaged on.

We sat on our swing in the warm evening and made last minute guesses as to what the card would say. It was a girl for sure. I mean, it had to be a girl, right? That's what we'd both been feeling the whole time.

Then, after months of *knowing* it was a girl, I suddenly panicked and realized that there was no reason why it couldn't be a boy. In fact, it probably was a boy. I had talked a girl up so much to myself that I started to feel a bit sad that instead I was going to have a boy. How many thoughts had I wasted on picturing myself braiding my daughter's hair, when in reality I should have been imagining telling my son to stop playing his drums so loud and to stop saying the word "fart."

"Well," Bill broke into my thoughts of bodily functions, "what are we waiting for?"

I took a big breath and slid my finger under the envelope to open it. My little handmade card stared back up at me as though we hadn't seen each other for months. The anxiety I had been feeling all day for this moment suddenly left me paralyzed and unable to open the card.

I collected myself and slowly peeled back the cover to reveal one simple word that made my pregnancy feel more real than I could ever imagine: GIRL.

Tears flowed out of complete joy, but also out of fear. I would have the awesome, yet daunting responsibility as the mother of a girl, to teach and show her as best I could from my own experience thus far how to find her own strong.

I immediately called my mom for guidance.

CHAPTER 29

Riding in a Soup Can Has Never Been so Sticky

Pregnancy is fun. Being pregnant with your sister and best friend? Fun times two. I'm very good at math.

Of all the hilarious experiences I've had with Meghan, and there were many, I think this one takes the cake.

One perfectly crisp autumn morning, we dragged our husbands to a fall festival. As a word of caution, if you choose to visit a pumpkin patch while hugely pregnant, you will get interrogated by at least 50% of the people there who think they're being funny by asking if you're smuggling out a pumpkin. I think this year, I actually *will* smuggle out a pumpkin in my shirt and people will just assume I'm pregnant. Joke's on all of you, plus hey, free pumpkin.

Baby or pumpkin? You'll never know. Mwah hah hah

This festival was so complex, it even had one of those tin trains for kids to ride in. You know what I'm talking about—the fantastically old metal ones with cars that look like giant empty soup cans turned on their sides.

Now imagine two full-grown (and fully-pregnant) women squeezing themselves into those little soup-can cars. It was not our wisest decision, but the train was practically empty, so Meghan and I asked if we could ride. The guy driving the rig replied that if we could get *into* the car, he'd take us around. So, we rode.

Hey, where'd my legs go?!

It was sheer bliss, feeling the wind in our faces and the sun on our backs. Like heaven really. But, then it stopped and we had to get out. Only, we couldn't.

Here are three things to keep in mind if you're ever considering going for this type of a train ride:

1. Soup-can cars are intended for children.
2. Soup-can cars are made of metal and aren't at all flexible, so if you get stuck, you're really stuck.
3. If you decide to ride in one despite my other points, at least remember not to wear slippery maternity jeans.

It took me a good several minutes to contort my way out of that thing. Thank goodness for prenatal yoga. In my own agony, I completely failed to remember how

Meghan's legs are significantly longer than mine and how her belly was a couple of months ahead of mine. Upon my escape, I found Meghan completely wedged into her soup can, not able to move an inch one way or the other.

To add to the scene, we emoted so much joy during our ride that several children ran up to wait for the next ride. So, the entire train quickly filled with eager children—except for one poor little kid who couldn't find an open seat because Meghan was stuck on the train.

Before long, an entire crowd had gathered around to see this fully pregnant woman jammed into the car. She should have gotten paid because clearly she had become the festival's main attraction. The more she tried to free herself, the more stuck she became. Our husbands got on either side of her and tried hoisting her up by her arms. Still no movement.

Like a true soldier, she hollered bravely to the driver, "Just start driving these poor kids around. I'll figure something out!" But, the mom of the boy without a seat would have none of that. Her son *needed* that soup can car emptied for him ASAP.

I was a terrible sister. I stood right next to her car and laughed my head off. I couldn't help it.

I laughed when the guy standing behind us said, "Whelp, looks like you bought yourselves a new train!" I laughed when the moms of all the kids waiting for the ride to start crossed their arms impatiently and sighed louder than needed. I laughed when I pictured Meghan getting pulled out of that thing with the Jaws of Life. I laughed when the driver did absolutely nothing, because he knew it was a lost cause, and plus it was giving a bit of entertainment to his otherwise boring work day. Shoot, I'm even laughing out loud right now as I'm writing this.

After a solid twenty minutes, and by some autumn miracle, Meghan finally freed herself from the terrible grasp of the soup can car. In the process, her stretchy maternity pants slipped down to a level that would embarrass even a high schooler used to wearing his jeans hanging off his butt. Her supportive husband's only comment was, "Don't worry, sweetie. I'm pretty sure I'm the only one you mooned." It was fantastic.

Her only battle wounds (other than a battered ego) were some fantastic bruises on her knees. At her next OB appointment, her doctors saw the bruises and immediately sounded the alarms to check Meghan's iron levels. Meghan just nodded and looked at the floor. She didn't have the guts to tell them that even the most iron-rich person in the world couldn't get out of that predicament without purpling up a little bit.

CHAPTER 30

Just When You Think it Can't Get Any Hippier

From day one, I knew how my pregnancy would end: me holding my screaming newborn wrapped in a blue and pink hospital swaddle, while the numbness from my epidural wore off. As everybody knows, that's just the way birth happens.

So, the first time I heard mention of something different, I couldn't help but to scoff. Why would anybody question or switch up a system that *works*? And then one day, my world came crashing down around me. Dramatic, right? Re: first world problems.

It all started when we were having dinner with some friends and a girl, who I didn't even know, asked me what my birth plan was. I had never even *heard* the term birth plan, so I was at a loss. But, of course I couldn't let her know that.

"Well," I stalled for time, trying to think of something that could maybe pass for intelligent on a topic I didn't even know existed. Then, pure inspiration hit me—one time while we were in Seattle watching *Grey's Anatomy* (because we had finished the entire *Dawson's Creek* collection), the doctor delivered a baby in a giant tub of water. It looked kind-of awesome in the same way that watching a circus contortionist shove himself into a box looks awesome; it's sort-of freaky and disgusting, but you can't stop staring.

"I've always thought a water birth sounded interesting..." I said with pure confidence, as though I'd been dreaming of a water birth since my own birth. Bill looked at me with a raised eyebrow, but I avoided his eye and stayed focused on my "birth plan."

The girl took the bait. She jumped right in with how *she* had wanted a water birth too, but couldn't have one at the hospital.

"Yeah," I consoled her, "that's rough, huh?" (As if I had any idea whether or not you could have a water birth at a hospital.)

"You should really watch this documentary called *The Business of Being Born*. It has some great examples of water births. I think you'd really like it." The title went in one ear and out the other. Why did I need to see more scenes of water births? *Grey's Anatomy* showed me all I needed to know. I still nodded enthusiastically at her suggestion, and didn't notice my husband typing the film information into his phone.

After our guests left that night, Bill pulled the video up on his computer and invited me to watch it with him. We sat down innocently, thinking we were only going to be watching a couple of women laboring in tubs, but instead we watched as Ricki Lake told us over and over again through stats and experiences why home births were far superior to hospital births.

I had to admit, the information shared *was* interesting and did make a lot of sense, but it didn't apply to me; I already knew I was having a happy, epidural-filled hospital birth. End of story.

I mean, who in the world would want to have a home birth in this day and age when all this modern technology exists to make birthing easier? Haven't we clearly advanced past the era of jamming a stick in a woman's mouth to stifle screaming while she delivered a baby by candlelight on a straw bed?

No, that was not for me. I was a modern day woman who deserved to be given the best possible care during my labor. So what if my other anticipated life plans had all fallen by the wayside, this plan would surely stick.

Bill didn't quite see it my way. During the end credits, he turned to me with his fist in the air and said, "HOME BIRTH ALL THE WAY, BABY!"

My inward reaction quickly went from,

"You're such a tease," to

"Wait, you're not kidding?" to

"Did you not see all that screaming and blood? Only the hospital knows how to truly handle that!" to

"If you were the one with an imminent birth in your near future, I bet you wouldn't be so quick to say that, Mister!" to

"How DARE you tell me how I should or shouldn't give birth. This has nothing to do with you!"

And then my outward reaction came in a single (passive-aggressive) statement, "I'm taking the dogs for a walk."

I had to get out of the house and into the cold night air, and quickly. The dogs had different plans, though. Milo planted himself in the front yard where he found something, most likely a dead animal, to roll around in, while Teddy wandered up and down our street aimlessly waiting for a car to come and hit him.

I screamed to no avail at the dogs with every ounce of frustration I was feeling. They both played dumb and went about their own agendas. I'm not trying to insinuate that this was anything out of the normal; our dogs often acted as ridiculous as this. But that night, I was in too fragile of a state to deal with it.

So, I started crying. I sobbed right there in my front yard while my dog bathed in the remains of some small carcass. I couldn't even control my dumb pet, how in the *world* was I supposed to make big decisions on how to have and raise a human child?

I ran back into the house, leaving the dogs outside to fend for themselves, and raced straight upstairs to our room. Bill followed closely but carefully behind me, and watched silently as I huffed around getting myself ready for bed. I didn't dare make eye contact with him for fear that the tears wouldn't stop.

I crawled into bed, rolled up into a tight ball and put out my best *don't touch me* sonar. Tears silently rolled onto my pillowcase as Bill cautiously laid down next to me.

Remember, I hadn't said a word to him at this point, so he had *no* idea what was going on with me. Why did I just snap? Was it safe for him to be in close quarters with me? Should he call in reinforcements just in case? I forever feel bad for guys in these situations.

After a couple of silent minutes, he curled up right against me and put his arms around me. There were no words that could have told him that's exactly what I needed him to do. I cried even more.

"What's up?" He asked tentatively.

The words came in one long, stringy, sobby breath, "I'm going to make a terrible mother. I can't even raise a dog right, how am I supposed to raise a kid? There are so many ways to screw up already and I haven't even had the baby yet. What if I give birth improperly? Who knew there were so many ways to do it. What if I do it all wrong?"

Bill hugged me tighter, "There are so many ways to do it *right*, too. Just trust yourself—not me or anybody else—and your intuition. This is gonna be one fun ride!" I love my husband.

The next morning, I woke up in much better spirits. I started off by revisiting the movie and recognizing that I could relate to a lot of what it was saying. In a hospital birth, women are usually forced to labor on their backs, which is not an ideal laboring position. Having my regular prenatal yoga class had convinced me that this was true—there were just some positions that felt better than others, and flat on my back was not one of them. I hadn't thought about it before, but it seemed true that back labor might not be that efficient.

I also liked to hear about the strong personal relationships most midwives and women form over the course of a pregnancy and delivery. Knowing first hand how cold doctors can be, I longed for that kind of personal attention from a caregiver.

More than anything though, the movie just made me feel uncomfortable in my naivety. I had no idea that most doctors today have never even seen a fully natural birth without drugs or interventions of any kind from beginning to end, let alone been actively a part of one. Isn't that kind-of scary?

Then, there was the talk about how comfortably and quickly doctors give drugs or make the unnecessary decision to perform a C-section simply because a labor was taking "too long." It made sense to me that, just like in every aspect of life, each labor and delivery are completely unique and special and deserve to be treated as such instead of being lumped into a "perfect birth" mold. Who's to say what "too long" is if everything appears otherwise healthy?

I was conflicted. The film definitely stirred up some things inside of me. I knew there were plenty of instances where a C-section or assisted birth was necessary and awesome, but were there just as many times when a woman's natural strength was ignored or denied for the sake of the clock? My body clearly knew how to grow a baby, shouldn't I trust it fully to also deliver a baby? I didn't want someone else making decisions about what I could and couldn't handle. On the other hand, a hospital birth just seemed so safe and *normal.*

I knew what my inner hippie needed that day to clear my mind: a good old yoga class. Boy had I shifted a lot from my days of studying for the LSAT. A new teacher smiled up at me when I walked into class, and I fell instantly in love with her. I'm not sure if it was her teaching or my mindset, or probably a combination of both, but I found myself feeling things I've never felt before in a yoga class.

If you've ever been to a yoga class, you know that instructors love to talk about breathing. Like any normal human being, I've always done a great job breathing during yoga because if I stopped breathing, I would die. But, also like most normal human beings, I had never mastered the art of *focusing* on my breath. Until that day.

It felt so clear to me that morning that I was breathing for someone else. Each breath was for my baby, and I asked with every inhalation how she wanted to come into this world. I know it sounds so cheesy, and maybe it is, but it helped me to clear my head. Even cheesier, I felt like my baby girl was prompting me with each exhalation to talk to the teacher about her kids.

So, after the class, I tried to casually ask the instructor if she had any kids of her own. I'm sure it sounded more creepy than casual, but I was doing my best.

"Two kids—four and six years old," she said quickly and went about her cleanup. Okay, now what?

Thankfully, one of other students took over from there, "Did you practice prenatal yoga during your pregnancies?"

"Yes, and it helped immensely with labor and delivery. I'm not just saying that to get you to come back to class."

I silently thanked the student for being more on her game than I and jumped back in with what I really wanted to know,

"So, did you deliver your kids naturally? No drugs or anything?"

"Yup. Actually, I had both of them at home." Bingo.

I couldn't help myself after that and started spilling my guts about how I had watched this movie and was freaking out. The instructor had nothing but glowing words to say about her experience with home birth and raved about how wonderful it is to be in your home right when your baby's born. She gave me the name and number of her midwife with high recommendations.

I left the yoga class oddly interested in calling this midwife. What in the world? What was wrong with me? Clearly, all that deep breathing in class had gone straight to my head.

Per usual whenever something out of the ordinary had entered into my life, I matched it up against all those checklists that had been already disproved so many times, but which still acted as my crutch. I was clearly not meant to have a home birth. I mean, home births were for earthy, über-buff women who were not afraid of getting their hands dirty. Definitely not for a straight-laced girl who couldn't even do a pushup.

Yet, there was something hugely appealing about the thought of being able to lay in my own bed to hold my baby seconds after her birth. To add to that cozy visual, my little girl was due at the end of December, so it would likely be snowing outside. Why would I want to brave the snow to drive to a hospital when I could be cuddled up in my own home? That sounded so nice and peaceful.

Plus, our house already held such great meaning for us as a family. From our house-hunting date, to Bill's surprise purchase, to our wedding party, our home had already been a huge backdrop in our life together. How cool if the birth of our daughter happened in that same sacred space?

Of course, the conservative voice in me shouted out again, "You are completely off your rocker! What if something goes wrong? Then what?!?"

"I don't know," my earthier side tried to sound brave, "we're not far from a hospital, so I don't see why we couldn't rush to one if needed."

"What about the pain? Sorry to burst your bubble, but there's no way you're getting an epidural at home."

"La, la, la, I'm not listening anymore!" There was no way I was tackling the painkiller part of things, yet.

In my head, this proved that I was still far from jumping on the home birth train. Chances were that we'd have our baby in the hospital, so setting up one measly, little midwife interview just for fun felt innocent enough.

And then, something magical happened. I finally felt like I was truly ready to find my own strong. I was ready to take total control of the situation without looking to somebody else for guidance or approval. I was ready to really, honestly look past the checklists and the boxes for good, and to make a choice that reflected my true self.

I felt empowered knowing that I could have the pregnancy and birth that *I* wanted instead of just going through the motions that the majority of our society goes through. I could do it *my* way and follow *my* path. And, for once, I didn't feel overwhelmed with the task of figuring that path out.

Just for comparison's sake, I set up two midwife interviews. Our first was with a lady named Flame. Yes, Flame. And yes, she was crazy. Fantastic, but crazy. Flame came into our home and immediately demanded a glass of water from Bill, putting extra emphasis on her viewpoint that men were here to serve women. I'm actually surprised she called him by his name instead of just snapping her fingers at him.

After receiving her water, and not drinking any of it before putting it on the table, she got right to work. Bill and I sat on the couch and motioned for her to sit, too, but she didn't. Instead, she started demonstrating all of the things that *I* should have been doing instead of sitting on a couch.

"Back in the day," she dramatically exclaimed, "women spent their days working in the fields and washing laundry. They lived on their knees." She got on her knees for emphasis and acted like she was weeding our hardwood floor. "They cleaned their baseboards and dirt floors day in and day out. Watch what happens when you're cleaning like that." She got on all fours and turned away from us. Then she started scrubbing our baseboards while wiggling her butt frantically like she was a duck learning to dance.

After a good, solid minute of that, she turned around and sat down on the floor while shouting out suggestions—no, not suggestions—DEMANDS for me to stay healthy during pregnancy. I sat with my mouth agape while Bill just laughed hysterically the entire time. From all the movies I've seen, I'm pretty sure servant boys are supposed to compose themselves better than that.

"She was energetic," Bill mused after she left.

I butt in with all the passion inside of me, "She will NOT be my midwife. Not in a million years! I feel stressed out after just having her in my home for 20 minutes. There's no way I could deliver a baby with her around!" I did silently admit that it was a very entertaining 20 minutes, though. Plus, now my baseboards were all clean.

Next we met with Elizabeth, the midwife my yoga teacher had used and recommended. In contrast to Flame, Elizabeth had an incredibly calm disposition and a very happy feel about her. Two seconds into our meeting with her, I went from expecting a hospital birth, to being absolutely certain that my baby would be born at home.

When Bill asked what Elizabeth's favorite part of being a midwife was, she described the awesomeness of getting to continually watch women go through the most intense transformation of their lives. Each woman starts off their pregnancy figuring out all these changes in her body and realizing that something huge is inevitable in her near future. Next, each woman turns back into her 7-year-old self, afraid of what's going to happen and unsure how it's even possible. Then, that little girl melts off along with a big chunk of selfishness as each woman surrenders her body and her life to this new little person she's had the great honor to create. Finally, of course, is the transition that comes with the labor and delivery. Each woman crosses the threshold into motherhood, where she learns to love in ways she never even knew were possible.

I could already feel some of this transition happening in my own body, so her description of it touched me. The part that really resonated for me, though, was how she emphasized that these things happened to *each woman*. It doesn't matter *how* the baby comes into this world, be it a medicated birth, home birth, or a C-section. Every woman has the equal opportunity to experience this transition; it's something that bonds all mothers across the world. I loved hearing that.

Of course, my sweet husband sat by my side and held my hand as these little snippets of transformation started to wash over me. To this day, I still feel that as hard as I try, I don't think I can ever fully express how truly grateful I am to have him in my life and to have a little family together.

And that's how I came to be that crazy hippie lady who birthed her children at home. I suddenly found myself subconsciously washing my baseboards on a regular basis.

CHAPTER 31

Don't Be Afraid to Stand Up for Your Path

So, there I was, 10 weeks till go-time with zero logged hours of baby-delivery practice or training. As any expectant mama can attest, it's an unnerving feeling.

At each appointment, Elizabeth helped to calm me down with a foot massage. That's right, people—a freakin' foot massage. When was the last time your doctor gave you that kind of service? That question doesn't apply if you consider a podiatrist "your doctor."

Outside of the regular foot massage (like anything else mattered), other differences in this meeting versus my doctor's appointments included: no waiting room, an *hour* long appointment, and an eagerly attentive caregiver. It felt wonderful, to say the least.

But, of course, all good massages must come to an end, and the reality would set back in. I had willingly signed up to push something the size of a small watermelon out of something the size of…well, not a watermelon, WITH NO PAIN MEDICATION. It seemed like an impossible-to-solve word problem that not even the smartest kid in the class got right.

In an effort to try to figure it out anyway, we not only took a crash course birthing class, but I also found ways in my daily life to *train* for birth. For example, Bill treated me to a prenatal massage once I started waddling instead of walking. Side note: if you have a pregnant friend, gift them a massage. They'll be your new best friend. If they're already your best friend, they'll be your old best friend with a new commitment to *stay* your best friend.

At one point during my massage, the therapist started to play with my ears. Uh, what?! I freaked out in my head for a couple of reasons. First, who in the world knew that an earlobe massage was a thing? Second, I hate/detest/loathe when anybody messes with my ears.

I'll admit it, I was born with ears that stick out. They were so big when I was a baby that my pediatrician recommended to my mom that she tape my ears to my head to help them form differently. I like to imagine my mom kicking that doctor in his nose and running out while holding Baby Me, big ears and all, screaming, "Thanks for nuttin' Doc!" I'm proud that she didn't tape my ears to my head and I secretly enjoy looking a little bit elfin.

I digress…It's an elf thing. The point is, I really don't like it when people mess with my ears, so I opened my mouth to put a stop to the ridiculous lobe rubbing. But, in a moment of enlightenment (or just brief insanity) I had the crazy thought that if I could push through this unenjoyable sensation, it would prove that I could also push through labor. For anybody who hasn't experienced labor, I'm sorry to tell you that it feels nothing like an ear massage. Don't say I didn't warn you.

When I wasn't training for birth, I started playing around with how it felt to *tell* people I was planning a home birth. And that's when I learned about a little pregnancy phenomenon called, *everybody gets up in your business*.

I actually think this happens whether or not you're pregnant, but it felt especially strong and pointed when I had a belly bump. Maybe it was just the extra emotions talking. But seriously, nobody in their right mind would ever just walk up to a non-pregnant woman and start rubbing her belly, right? I rest my case.

The first time I said the word "home birth" aloud in a group was during somebody else's baby shower. One woman asked the guest of honor where she was giving birth. This is apparently a normal question to ask, which I did not know pre-pregnancy.

The pregnant girl said, "Well, duh. At the hospital." Maybe she wasn't so rude about it; the memory is hazy. Then, the questioner turned to me, the other expectant lady in the room, and asked me the same thing. If I had any clue the riot my answer would cause, I would have kept my mouth shut. The entire room fell completely silent. Let me tell you, a room full of women with no one talking is a very unnerving thing.

Then, someone broke the silence. You'd think the end of an uncomfortable silence would be a welcome sound, but I would definitely take the silence over the questions that shot at me.

"Don't you realize the risks involved with birth?"

"Are you crazy?"

"You could die without medical help!"

"We have hospitals for a reason…"

The questions sounded different, but when you boil them all down, they were each saying the same thing: "Your body doesn't know what to do on its own."

And then the horror stories started. Everybody knew somebody who had a birth that would have gone really sour if they hadn't been in a hospital. The rest of the lovely baby shower was spoiled—all thanks to me. Sorry about that, guest of honor.

On one hand, I wanted to curl up in the corner and suck my thumb. Why was everyone being so mean about a decision that had nothing to do with them? On the other hand, I wanted to scream at the top of my lungs, "MY BODY DOES KNOW WHAT TO DO! IT'S GOTTEN ME THIS FAR, HASN'T IT?!"

From then on, I wanted to wear a sign that said, "Attention world: I appreciate your concern for my safety and the well-being of my baby, I really do, but please butt-out of my business. This decision was not made lightly and more importantly, was made by *me* and concerns only *me*."

I felt insanely confident of the path I was treading, and knew more than ever that my strength would never come from trying to fit into a mold. My strength, and the true strength possessed by others, comes when we stand up for our personal beliefs. Even if the majority of people around me had scoffed at my plan, it suited me perfectly. This attitude, by the way, does not only apply during pregnancy. Regardless of what you're doing, your strength will come when you stand up for what you personally believe.

And, speaking from experience, when you find that strength, you will feel like an immortal goddess.

CHAPTER 32

Warning: Labor Story Ahead

I'll try my best to keep my birth story short and clean for those of you with either an intolerance to blood, or an intolerance to birth stories.

I was in my bedroom talking to my belly, because that's what you do when you're pregnant (or insane). "Don't feel rushed," I told my baby, "but we're ready for you to come whenever you want." I quickly learned after having children that mildly *suggesting* they do something is a worthless parenting approach that leads to zero productivity, and often tears. Sometimes even from the kids.

But, in this instance, my little girl obediently heard my suggestion and said, "Whelp, better now than never. It's go time!" She was born with very advanced conversational skills.

Literally minutes after that verbal exchange with my belly, my abdomen started to tighten. Was this it? I knew not to freak out because Elizabeth had drilled into my head that most labor starts with early labor; the phase that could last several hours and be only mildly uncomfortable.

During early labor, a mama should try to distract herself by watching a movie or going grocery shopping. My set plan was to fill up my *birthing tub* during this phase so that I'd be able to labor in the water, just like my fake birth plan indicated that I'd wanted to do back when I thought having a baby at home only existed in the dark ages and soap operas.

The intensity I was feeling…intensified. I called for Bill as calmly as I could. Similarly prepped about early labor, Bill sauntered upstairs with his laptop, hopped into bed, and checked in with me before continuing to do some work.

These sensations were not slowing down, though. I panicked and thought, "If I'm supposed to be able to watch a movie right now, there's no *way* I'm going to be able to handle the next phases of labor."

I couldn't lie down anymore with the contractions rolling through me. People talk about how labor brings women into their fully animal state. I proved that to be true when I positioned myself on my hands and knees, and didn't move for an entire nine hours.

At that point, Bill knew it was time to call Elizabeth, who quickly determined that I had completely skipped over early labor and was already well into active labor. I focused everything I could onto my breathing, which kept me grounded and loose. Thanks, prenatal yoga, I owe you one.

If you look up "natural birth" videos on YouTube (trust me, I did), there's a similarity to any one you watch that can seem almost fake and even a little bit funny. What's with all these seemingly possessed moaning women? I would certainly *not* be doing that during my birth, thank you very much. Yet, there I was in the middle of the action, mooing like a dying cow. So much for absolute statements.

Even in my animalistic state, I was very aware of Bill's presence the entire time. I felt more love for him in those hours than I had ever felt for anyone before. He stayed right by my side and supported me through every contraction. There were no nurses pushing him away from me to check my vitals, or machines blocking our connection. It was just him and me in a profoundly intimate moment, preparing for this new chapter to begin.

When Elizabeth did arrive, I worried that she would poke and prod at me and maybe even make me change my position, which I very much did not want. Aside from quickly putting a stethoscope up to my belly to check the baby's heartbeat, she did nothing of the sort. She stood back in all of her gloriously calm energy, and told me I was doing everything perfectly. She could tell just by my breathing and my demeanor that things were fine.

Not to sound completely ethereal, but the feeling in our bedroom that night was perfect. My sweet husband brought a sensitivity, life, and vitality to the room that I'll never forget. To compliment it, Elizabeth brought an incredibly gentle spirit that was just right. I felt an overwhelming amount of gratitude knowing that my new little baby girl's first exposure to this crazy world was going to be so full of calmness, warmth, and love.

Even though it was intense, my entire labor felt like it had only lasted about 20 minutes. Our baby girl was born at exactly 9:00 in the morning. Bill got to catch her and be the first person to touch this brand-new little being. Nobody took her away from me to cut her cord or check her stats. Instead, I rolled over and held her close on my chest immediately, feeling her sweet warmth, and hearing that beautiful first cry. She was hands down the most perfect thing I had ever seen in my entire life. Words could never describe the love I instantly felt for my little girl.

Bill lay down next to us and everything in the world made so much more sense. This was what life was all about. Forget the checklists, forget the stereotypes…feeling that pure love trumped it all.

Elizabeth left us to bond as a family and went downstairs to make us breakfast in bed. She made me a four-egg omelet. A gourmet freaking *omelet*, people. I devoured that thing like I hadn't eaten in days, then curled up further into my own bed, and for the millionth time, thanked the Universe for bringing the idea of a home birth into my life.

I had changed from a girl to a woman in those nine hours. The ironic thing was the transition had nothing to do with my thoughts or plans. Here I had spent my life composing little checklists and ideals on how to become a strong woman, yet all I needed to do was to get out of my head and surrender to the natural flow intended for me in life. I needed to be the Pisces I was born to be.

In that moment of realization and acceptance, I was the strongest woman on the face of the earth.

CHAPTER 33

Be Yourself; Everyone Else is
Already Taken. ~ Oscar Wilde

So, there it is. Years and years of searching for my strong, and I found it with the help of a tiny little baby.

While I had every intention of continuing to run my event planning practice after my daughter was born, I found it to be my absolute least favorite part of the day; so I stopped working—just like that. All of my life-path speculations, calculations, and revisions that had once dictated my every waking hour suddenly seemed so trivial. At this juncture in my life, I was not meant to be defined by my career.

So, I willingly gave up my career ambitions to enjoy the opportunity to stay at home full time with my little rascals. And, I haven't regretted it for a single day. I'm now the proud mama of three little girls, all born at home with equally magical pregnancies and birth stories.

I love bustling around my kitchen and cooking something daily. I'm still no Julia Childs, but maybe someday. I keep a thriving vegetable garden where my produce has dared to grow bigger than a thimble. And,

I've accepted that I *can* sew as long as I don't have to follow any directions. My days are filled with laughter, snot, craft projects, tears, and many many conversations with my girls about what it means to be strong.

Is this my perfect path? Yes, it is for now. Is this everybody's perfect path? No.

That's the magic of it all: What's right for one person isn't at all right for another. And, it will change and evolve throughout your life. There are plenty of women out there who *are* the kickass career holders, and my hat goes off to them. There are also plenty of girls who choose to be mamas *and* business women, and that's amazing, too. There are others who aren't meant to be mamas at all, and that is equally awesome. I could go on and on, but for the sake of brevity, let me just say that the number of possibilities is endless. The point is, it's *your* life and it's *your* choice. If you love gardening, then garden. If you hate yoga, then don't do yoga. If you're good at baking, then please come to my house and teach me.

Don't let somebody else tell you what to do or try to fit you into a mold. Heck, don't even try to fit yourself into a mold, because there is no set mold that can house the awesomeness in store for you. You can write down all the life-path plans you want, but be open to the very real possibility that your true path might hit you upside the head when you're least expecting it. Be open to that.

Most importantly, be true to yourself, find your own flow, and own your own strong. That's where you'll find your real happiness.

Of course, don't take my word for it. After all, I still can't do a single pushup.

Acknowledgements

A huge thanks to everyone who helped make this memoir a reality for me.

First and foremost to my husband, Bill, who inspires and encourages me every single day. You wouldn't be reading this book if it wasn't for him supporting me through it all.

To my parents. You also wouldn't be reading this book if it wasn't for them, because I wouldn't be here. I also wouldn't be half the person I am without their awesome influence and teachings.

To my siblings. Meghan, for being my partner in crime, life support, and sounding board. Dustin, for being my childhood partner in crime, life support, and comic relief.

To my daughters, who are my everything. My life story didn't truly begin until they showed up.

To everyone who helped put this book together: Neil Robertson for sitting down early on and walking me through his processes in writing books (which I used religiously). Pat Concodora for editing and acting as my mentor as I entered the realm of authorship. Kelly Angelovic for creating the most perfect cover I could have imagined. All my friends who kept nudging and asking me for book updates to help keep me motivated. Kristen Gray for watching my daughters so I actually had time to write. And Panera Bread for providing me my favorite writing nook.

I love you all!!

www.ingramcontent.com/pod-product-compliance
Lightning Source LLC
Chambersburg PA
CBHW020613300426
44113CB00007B/621